Active Science 2

**Mike Coles
Richard Gott
Tony Thornley**

COLLINS
EDUCATIONAL

Collins Educational, 8 Grafton Street, London W1X 3LA

First published 1989

ISBN 0 00 327432 2

Designed by Wendi Watson

Artwork by Ray Burrows, Gay Galsworthy, Mike Gordon, Sally Neave

Printed and bound by Wing King Tong Ltd, Hong Kong

Acknowledgements

The authors and publishers are grateful to the following for permission to reproduce photographs on the pages indicated.

(T = top, B = bottom, M = middle, L = left, R = right)

Allsport 18L, Bob Martin 18R, 114, Simon Bruty 19, 32MR, 114TR
Ardea/John Mason 69TM, 80TM
Art Directors Photo Library 66, 67TL
Associated Press 81
Associated Sports Photography 112BL
Clive Barda/London 67BR
Barnaby's Picture Library 32TL, 38ML, 44BR, 53, 60, 78R, 128L, 134TL & R
Biophoto Associates 14TL, 108L
British Petroleum 37R, BP Research 51
Camera Press/Benoit Gysembergh 65
J. Allan Cash 32ML & TR, 38TL, TR, BL, BR, 44TM, 47, 68MR, 69MR, 71ML, 64R, 68, 69TL, 71L, 83, 86TR, 87, 88, 92T, 103, 112TL, 117, 118L
Central Electricity Generating Board 50TR, 52
Michael Cole 118R
Bruce Coleman/Hans Reinhard 63TL, 80TL
Mary Evans Picture Library 97, 101BL
Friends of the Earth 82MR
Geological Museum 132L & R
Sally and Richard Greenhill 75
GSF Picture Library 44TL, 86ML, 126, 132M
Dr T. H. Grenby/Guy's Hospital 14B, 15
Guardian/Ian Swift 77
Gyproc Insulation Ltd 48
Halfords 122
Robert Harding Picture Library 45B, 50ML, R. Adeney 110TR
Alan Hinkes 18M
ICCE Photo Library 37L
ICI 94, ICI Fibres 130TR
Frank Lane Picture Agency/H. Schrempp 63TR, Silvestris 63TM, Gardner 63BR, Wisniewski 128M, Wilmshurst 128R Dr de Zylva 135TR

London Scientific Films/Oxford Scientific Films 14TR
London Zoo 134BL & BR
Lucas Yuasa Batteries Ltd 80TR
Meat Marketing Board 44TR
Metropolitan Police 69TL, 115
NASA 105
NHPA/Stephen Dalton 32BL, 45T, 135BR
North of Scotland Hydro-Electric Board 50TL
Northwich Salt Museum 95T
Permutit Ltd 99BL
Peugeot Talbot 34B
Post Office 104L
Rex Features 67TR, Pascal Despeaux 101BR
Ann Ronan Picture Library 25, 58L, 69BL, 104R
St Bartholomew's Hospital, London 71R
Science Photo Library 28, 130TL & BM/CNRI 24L, Tektoff-RM/CNRI 24R, Sandoz/D. Zagury/Petit Format 26, PIR-CNRI 27, Cecil H. Fox 29T, Martin Dohrn 29B, Martin Bond 50BL, John Sanford 64L, Arnold Fisher 95B, James Stevenson 109, Earl Scott 124L, NASA 124R
W. A. Sharman 35
Ronald Sheridan 90
Liz Somerville 32BM
Tony Thornley 34T, 80B, 82B, 84B, 85T, 86B, 92B, 102B, 108R, 121, 123, 141
Topham Picture Library 76
Matthew Wilson and Andrew Thornley 59
Zefa/B. Julian 32BR, 112TR, 113, R. Sawade 135BL
Zoological Society 134TM, 135TL

Commissioned photography by Nance Fyson

Cover
Clockwise from top right: J. Allan Cash Photo Library, University of Durham School of Education, J. Allan Cash Photo Library, Barnaby's Picture Library, Frank Lane Picture Agency.

Contents

What it takes for you to be good at science

There are five areas you need to cover to be good at science.

Communicating and interpreting

Communicating

You should be able to:

- read tables, pie charts, bar charts and line graphs and know what they mean.
- pick out important pieces of information from books, magazines and worksheets.
- find patterns in tables, pie charts, bar charts and line graphs.
- describe clearly an experiment you have done.

Observing

Observing

You should be able to:

- pick out the important things about an object (and ignore other things).
- find similarities in a group of objects.
- find differences among the objects in a group.

Planning investigations

Planning

You should be able to:

- design an investigation to solve a problem.
- decide what equipment to use.
- decide what measurements to take.
- decide how the results would give an answer to the problem.

Investigating and making

You should be able to:

- decide what a problem means and how to solve it.
- set up and try out suitable apparatus.
- alter the investigation if it does not give an answer to the problem.
- use the results to work out an answer.
- decide when you need to do more experiments to check your results.

Basic skills

You should be able to:

- make tables of results.
- draw pie charts, bar charts and line graphs.
- know when to use each type of graph or chart.
- read measuring instruments as accurately as necessary.
- follow instructions for doing experiments.

You will get plenty of chances to practise these skills. Each chance for testing a skill is marked in this book with a coloured box.

 means there is a worksheet to go with the topic.

Safety symbols

You will find these signs used in the book. This is what they mean:

This sign is warning you that there are hazards here. You must take great care.

This sign tells you that you must protect your eyes by wearing special glasses.

EYE PROTECTION
MUST BE WORN

7·1 Why eat?

Food and drink

Your body is an incredible chemical factory. Without food and drink, it would stop working.

Food helps it to grow, to stay healthy and to keep active.

Drinks stop your body cells from drying out. They also carry all the other chemicals around your body.

Water is particularly important. About two thirds of you is water.

1 Are other plants and animals the same?

Planning

Water in living things

● Design an investigation to compare the amount of water in a piece of plant and the amount of water in a piece of meat.

● Before you start, plan the investigation in your book:

> 10/9/99 <u>Comparing water in living things</u>
>
> <u>Plan:</u>
>
> <u>What I will change:</u>
>
> <u>What I will measure:</u>
>
> <u>How I will measure it:</u>
>
> <u>What I will keep the same to make sure it is a fair test:</u>

● Ask your teacher to check your group's plan. Then try your investigation out.

● When your experiment is over, put in your book:
  – what you did.
  – what your results were.
  – what the results tell you.
  – how you altered your plan (if at all).

2 Do you have more water in you per hundred grams of your body weight than a plant does?

3 Do you think this answer is true for *all* plants?

What is in food?

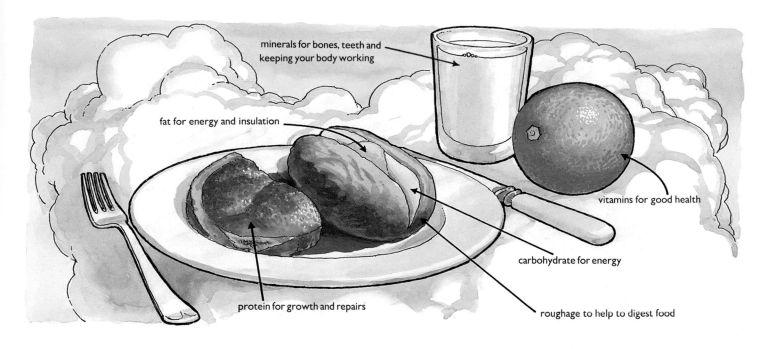

minerals for bones, teeth and keeping your body working

fat for energy and insulation

vitamins for good health

carbohydrate for energy

protein for growth and repairs

roughage to help to digest food

Testing food

Nutrients, like protein and carbohydrate, are the important things in your diet. You can test your own food for nutrients.

How to test for protein
- Mix a little of the food with water in a test tube.
- Add 2–3 drops of blue biuret reagent. Any protein in the food will turn the biuret reagent purple.

How to test for carbohydrates
Glucose
- Mix a little of the crushed food with water in a test tube.
- Add a few drops of blue Benedict's solution. (**Care!** It's poisonous.)

- Stand the test tube in boiling water for 5 minutes. Any glucose in the food will turn the solution green, then red.

Starch
- Take a small amount of the food and put on three drops of brown iodine solution. Any starch in the food will turn the iodine black.

How to test for fat
- Rub a little of the food on a piece of brown paper or greaseproof paper. Any fat in the food will leave a greasy stain on the paper.

Use the tests to answer some of these questions.

4 What nutrients are there in crisps?
5 Which foods in your school canteen contain protein?

6 Which drink contains most nutrients?
7 Are there any foods that contain all four of the nutrients listed?
- Present your group's results in a clear chart or table.

EXTRAS

1 Keep a record of everything you eat and drink for 24 hours. Use the worksheet to work out how much of each of the main nutrients you have eaten. Put your results in a table.

2 How do you think you could improve your diet?

1kJ means one thousand joules of energy. You will use up about 10 000 joules or 10kJ of energy in the time you take to read this page!

● Make a bar chart of the amount of energy that different people use. Put them in order so that the people who use the least energy come first.

● Choose any three people on your chart. For each one, explain why you think they use the energy that they do.
● Make a guess about the amount of energy that these people use each day. Explain your guess for each one:
  – your mum or dad.
  – a male teacher who does no exercise.
  – a female doctor who goes jogging.

1 Do women need more or less energy than men? Why is there a difference?

A healthy diet

A healthy diet gives you all the nutrients you need:
– enough energy to keep you going.
– enough protein for building and mending your body.
– enough vitamins and minerals to keep your body healthy.
– enough liquid to stop you drying out.

● Look back at the record you kept of your diet for 24 hours. Work out the total amount of energy that the food you ate gave you. (Worksheet 7.1 will help you.)

2 Did you eat enough energy food to cover the energy you used up?

3 What if you eat more than you need? Where does the extra go?

Food types

A 'square' meal should contain each of these four food types:

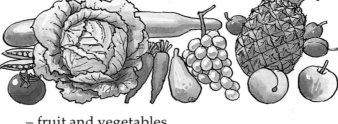

– fruit and vegetables

– main food (cheese/meat/fish/eggs/milk)

– fillers (bread/potatoes/pasta/cake/pudding)

– drinks

4 How many of your meals in the last week have been 'square'?

5 How many children in your class had a 'square' meal for their last school lunch?

● Work out a 'square' meal lunch for a child who has sandwiches. Find out the energy value of the meal. (Use worksheet 7.1 to help you.)

EXTRAS

Investigating

1 Do an investigation at home to find out what types of food birds prefer.

2 Make a table that shows what you were doing for every minute in the last 24 hours. Use worksheet 7.2A to fill in how much energy you used doing these things. Make a guess if what you did is not in the table. Does your total come to the right amount for your age and sex?

3 Worksheet 7.2B gives some incomplete meals. Complete it so that each of the meals is 'square'.

4 Do a survey of children during a lunch break. Count the number who have a 'square' meal. Keep a record of the number of items each of the other meals is missing.

5 You have got £5 to buy a balanced meal for a family of four. What would you buy? Why?

9

7·3 Additives and treatments

Adding things to food

Many things are added to our food and drink. These additives do several jobs:
– they colour food.
– they keep it fresh.
– they stop it from separating.
– they make it taste different.

Most additives are marked on the label of the food with an 'E number'.

E numbers

E100 to E180 are colourings. These are used to make the food look nicer. Many are natural colours and are not artificial chemicals.

E200 to E290 are preservatives. These are used to stop microbes growing in the food. Microbes make food go bad, and can make you very ill.

E300 to E321 are anti-oxidants. These stop oxygen in the air from making the food go bad.

CHEDDAR CHEESE SPREAD

INGREDIENTS: CHEDDAR CHEESE RECONSTITUTED SKIMMED MILK POWDER. BUTTER. WHEY POWDER. EMULSIFYING SALT (E339). SALT. PRESERVATIVE (E202). COLOUR. (E160e).

CHERRYADE
SUPER CONCENTRATE

INGREDIENTS

Water, sugar, citric acid, flavouring, artificial sweetener (sodium saccharin), preservative (E211), colours (E122, E124).

Beef Stock Cubes

Ingredients: Hydrolysed protein, wheatflour, yeast extract, salt, colour (caramel), beef stock, flavour enhancer (621, 635), beef fat, beef extract, sugar, vegetable oil, lactic acid, pepper, onion powder.

Wholemeal Bread

INGREDIENTS (in order of weight): WHOLEMEAL FLOUR, WATER, SALT, YEAST DRIED GLUCOSE SYRUP, VINEGAR, HYDROGENATED VEGETABLE OIL, EMULSIFIERS: E471, E472(e): FLOUR IMPROVER: L-ASCORBIC ACID. For SELL BY date see bag closure or label. Best within two days of purchase. If freezing place in deep freeze on day of purchase, use within three months.

READY SALTED FLAVOUR CRISPS

INGREDIENTS:
Potatoes, Vegetable Oil, Salt.

NUTRITIONAL INFORMATION
TYPICAL VALUES

	Per 100g	Per Pack
FAT (of which	36.8 g	9.2 g
Saturates)	14.3 g	3.6 g
PROTEIN	6.5 g	1.6 g
CARBOHYDRATE	40.1 g	10.0 g
ENERGY		
- kJoules	2184	546
- kcal	520	130
DIETARY FIBRE	11.9 g	3.0 g
SALT	1.12 g	0.28 g

Steakhouse Beef Grill

INGREDIENTS
Beef (minimum 95%).
Salt, Flavouring, Potato Starch. Sugar. Dextrose. Preservative (E223)

Produce of the United Kingdom

Beetroot

Ingredients: Beetroot, water, acetic acid, spirit vinegar, sugar, artificial sweetener (saccharin).

Other things added to food include:

– **emulsifiers and stabilisers** (between E322 and E494). These stop foods like mayonnaise from separating into different parts.

– **flavourings and flavour enhancers.** These make the food taste different. Some do not have E numbers (e.g. pepper), but others do. One common flavour enhancer is monosodium glutamate, E621. This is often used in things like sausages and instant dried meals.

– **sweeteners** (E420 and E421). Many sweeteners, like sugar, do not have an E number.

---

1 Which of the foods above has the most additives?

2 Which additive is most common in the foods shown?

3 Choose one of the foods above. Which of the additives in it *need* to be there? Why?

4 Which additives do *not* need to be there? Why do you think they are there?

Treating food

Food must be kept fresh. Adding a preservative is one way of doing this, but there are other ways.

In this experiment you have to find a way to stop milk from going off.

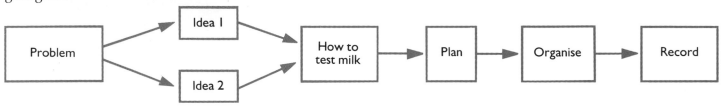

The problem
How can we find a way to keep milk fresh?

Some ideas

Idea 1: Heat
Milk is pasteurised by being heated to 70°C for a minute, then being cooled quickly.
Milk is sterilised by boiling.

Idea 2:
E223 (Campden tablets) preserves orange squash.
Vinegar and sugar are both preservatives.

How to test milk
– Tasting sour milk is **dangerous!** ⚠
– Milk that has gone off smells bad.
– Resazurin is a dye that is sensitive to sour milk. 1cm³ of Resazurin should be added to 10cm³ of milk. The dye goes from blue (in fresh milk) to pink (in just-off milk) to clear (in bad milk).

Plan
– Decide how many samples of milk you will work with.
– Decide how you will treat the samples to preserve them.
– Remember to have a 'control' – a sample that is not treated.
– Decide how often you will test your samples.
– Decide where you will keep the samples.
– Get your plan checked by your teacher.

Organise
– Collect the fresh milk.
– Divide it into samples.
– Treat each sample, and label it.
– Test a little of each sample straight away.
– Record your experiment and the results.
– Remember to test the samples every day for a few days.

Record
– Write up your results.
– Say what you think the best treatment is.
– Explain your ideas.

EXTRAS
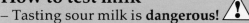

Observing

1 Have a careful look around your kitchen or a shop. Can you see different ways in which foods are preserved? Make a list. For each one say how it is preserved.

2 Choose ten foods in your kitchen at home. Make a table like the one shown and fill it in:

Food	Additives in the food	What the additives do	How long the food keeps fresh

7·4 Food processing

Where the food goes

6 p.m. Leila sits down to tea:
– cheese flan (mainly protein), salad and a
  baked potato (mainly starch)
– treacle pudding (mainly carbohydrate)
– a cup of tea

Mouth

Teeth chew the food and mix it with saliva.
Saliva helps to dissolve the starch in the
potato. It also makes the food easier to
swallow.

Oesophagus

6.20 p.m. The last lump of food is eaten. It
goes down the oesophagus to the stomach in
a few seconds.

Stomach

7.00 p.m. The food is mixed with acid
juices which kill microbes in the food. Other
chemicals help to dissolve the food.
Carbohydrates, such as starch, dissolve fast;
fats take longer to dissolve.

Small intestine

12.00 midnight Now the food is all in the
small intestine. It is a thick milky mixture.
More chemicals are added from the liver and
pancreas.

Some of the dissolved food passes through
the wall of the small intestine into the blood.

The small intestine is about six metres
long. By the time the food has got through it,
all the useful nutrients have passed into the
blood.

Appendix

In humans, the appendix does not do a
useful job. The food does not stay in it. But
in many animals the appendix is used to
digest grass and other plants that humans
cannot eat.

Large intestine

6.00 a.m. Water is taken out of the
undigested fibre and other waste. The solid
waste passes into the rectum. The water
passes into the bladder.

Rectum and anus

6.00 p.m. When the rectum is full, the
waste is ready to pass out of the anus. The
waste is called faeces.

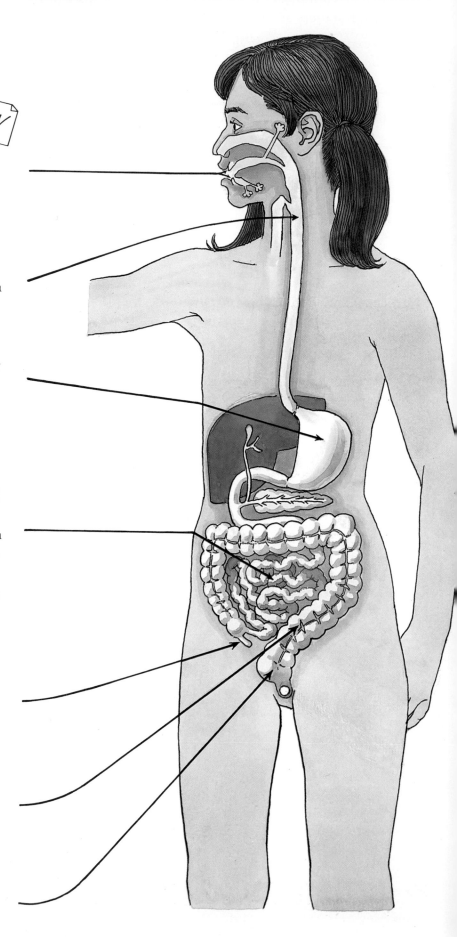

● Draw a flow chart that shows how your lunch yesterday passed through your body. Name each part it went through. Say what happens at each place.

1 Which parts of Leila's meal have been absorbed into her blood? Where has the rest gone?

Saliva at work

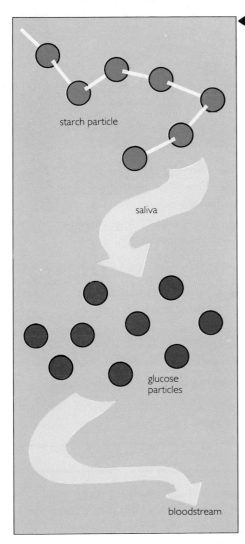

starch particle

saliva

glucose particles

bloodstream

Your saliva helps to break up large starch particles into glucose. Glucose particles can pass into your blood stream because they are small. Starch particles cannot: they are too big.

● Your group has to find out how quickly saliva works.

First, plan your experiment and get your plan approved.

● Look back at 7.1 to see how to test for glucose.
● Bread is a good starchy food to test.
● Your teacher will give you some saliva to use (you can dilute it with some water if you want).
● You should try giving the saliva between 0 and 20 minutes with the bread.
● Remember that in your mouth the saliva is kept warm. This helps the saliva to work.
● **Don't put any bread or saliva in your mouth!** ⚠️
● Carry out your experiment, and write up your results.

● If you have time, find out:
– if saliva works better as it gets warmer.
– if 'chewing' helps saliva to work. **Do not** ⚠️ **do this in your mouth!**
– if there are any 'energy' foods that saliva cannot turn into glucose.

EXTRAS

1 Did Leila have a balanced meal? How could her meal be improved?

2 Draw a time line down the side of a page in your exercise book. Mark 6.00 p.m. at the top, 7.00 p.m. on the next line down, 8.00 p.m. on the next line, until the end of the page. Write down what happened to Leila's meal next to the right time on your page.

3 What do you think goes wrong in your digestive system:
(a) when you are sick (vomit)?
(b) when you have diarrhoea?

7·5 Teeth

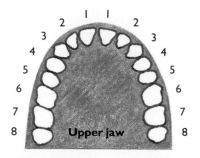

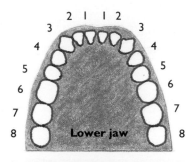

Upper jaw

Lower jaw

1, 2 incisor

3 canine

4, 5 pre-molar

6–8 molar

The diagram shows a full set of human teeth.

1 How many teeth does a healthy adult have?

2 How many teeth of each type does he or she have?

Observing

Now answer these questions in your book:

These teeth are from the front of a sheep's mouth. They are called incisors.

3 What do sheep use these teeth for? (Think about what they eat.)

4 Which teeth in your mouth are like this?

These teeth are from the back of a sheep's jaw. They are called molars.

5 What do you think a sheep uses these teeth for?

6 Which teeth in your mouth are like this?

The pointed teeth in a tiger's mouth are called canine teeth.

7 What does a tiger use its canine teeth for? (Think about what it eats.)

8 Which teeth in your mouth are like this?

- Draw a side view of one tooth of each type in your mouth. Next to the drawing write down what type of tooth it is, and what its job is.
- Count how many teeth of each type your friend has.
- Put the results on a tooth chart, or make a sketch of your friend's mouth.

Getting it straight

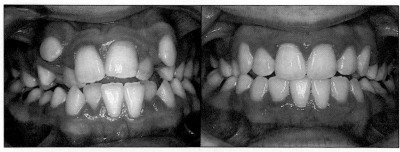

Mike's teeth before straightening.

Mike's teeth 21 months later.

Many children have crooked teeth or overcrowded mouths. A special dentist called an orthodontist gets their teeth right. She may have to remove some teeth, or get the child to wear a brace. Her work is helped by the child's tongue and lips because they help keep teeth straight.

- Make a list of the changes you can see in Mike's teeth.

9 Has Mike had any teeth taken out?

10 Which of his teeth have been straightened?

Keeping teeth healthy

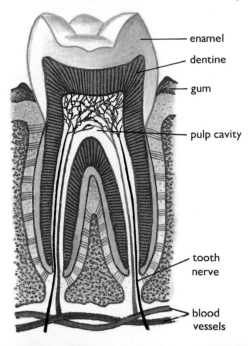

enamel
dentine
gum
pulp cavity
tooth nerve
blood vessels

Enamel is the hardest substance in your body. It is not living material, and it is not replaced by the body.

Dentine is like bone. It is not as tough as enamel, but it is replaced by the body.

The blood supply and nerves let the tooth live and grow.

When you eat, tiny pieces of food stay on your teeth and gums. Microbes on your teeth change the food into acids that attack the enamel. Once the enamel layer has gone, the dentine wears away quickly. It leaves the nerve exposed and you get toothache.

You can stop this decay by brushing your teeth properly and regularly. Brushing removes plaque, which is a mixture of food, microbes and acid.

You can see the plaque in your mouth if you use a disclosing tablet. This dyes plaque a bright colour. Look at the teeth below, which have been dyed three times:
– once after a meal
– once after brushing normally
– once after brushing carefully

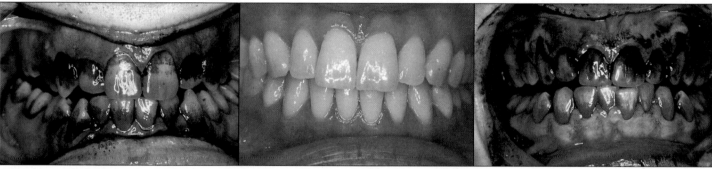

11 Which photo do you think is which?

Work in a team with your friends.
● Make a list of the things you should do when you brush your teeth. Think about:
– time taken to brush
– direction of brushing
– toothpaste
– how often you brush

● Do a survey in your group to find out how often and how long each person brushes his or her teeth.

EXTRAS

Planning

1 Imagine that you have to find out which of two types of toothbrush is best for cleaning teeth. Write a plan for an investigation that you could do.

2 (a) Mark on a tooth chart the fillings in your teeth or your parents' teeth.
(b) Find out what fillings are made from.
(c) What does a dentist want a material for fillings to be like? Make a list of all the properties that are important.

3 Find out why fluoride is added to some water supplies, and to some toothpastes. Why do you think that some people do not want fluoride in the water supply?

4 Make a poster that explains to six-year-olds how to care for their permanent teeth.

Fitness means

because . . .

1

breathing easily after exercise

* A fit person's lungs get air in and out smoothly.
* They have a large capacity.
* The air channels in the lungs are not blocked.
* Oxygen can get into the blood easily.

2

keeping going

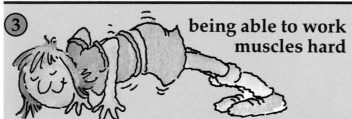

* Muscles need oxygen and glucose to work. These are carried to the muscles by the blood.
* A fit body has a healthy heart to pump the blood.
* The blood vessels must not be blocked up.

3

being able to work muscles hard

* Muscles need a good blood supply to provide fuel and to remove waste.

4

bending and stretching easily

* Muscles are kept healthy by being used.
* The other tissues in your body (ligaments that hold the bones together, and tendons that join muscle to bone) need to be kept supple.
* Regular exercise keeps the tissues strong and flexible.

5

staying healthy

* Fit people do get ill, but they usually recover faster than unfit people.
* Fit people make sure their bodies get what they need – for example by eating a good diet.
* Fit people avoid unhealthy habits like smoking.

6

feeling good

* You feel good if you are healthy.

How fit are you? ⚠️

1 How deeply can you breathe?

- Survey your friends: find out how many breaths each one takes in a minute.
- Then let them try the same thing after doing step-ups for a minute.

1 Does the breathing rate change? Why?

Fitter people have a smaller change in breathing rate.

How much air can you hold in your lungs?

- Blow up a plastic bag as far as you can with one breath.
- Then squeeze the air into a beaker full of water in a plastic bowl.

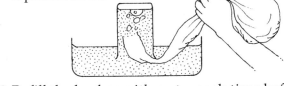

- Refill the beaker with water each time before you fill it with air.
- Work out the capacity of your lungs.

2 Do girls have better lungs than boys?

2 What is your pulse rate?

- Find the pulse on your wrist.
- Count how many beats it does in a minute. This is measuring your heart rate. It should be about 60 to 80 beats per minute.
- Do sit-ups or step-ups for 1 minute.
- Measure your pulse rate again for 1 minute.
- Measure it again after 5 minutes' rest.

Fit people have a low resting pulse rate. Their pulse rate goes down quickly after exercise.

- Design and carry out an experiment with your friends to see who has the fittest heart.

3 How fit are your leg muscles?

- Do a standing broad jump to find out who has the strongest legs.
- Find out if tall people jump further.

4 How supple is your body?

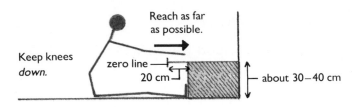

Reach as far as possible.
Keep knees *down*.
zero line
20 cm
about 30–40 cm

- Hold this position for 3 seconds, then measure the distance from the 0 line.
- Find out if girls are more supple than boys.
- This test measures how supple your trunk and hips are. Try to design a test for arms and shoulders.

5 How good is your stamina?

(**Hint:** Practise first getting the rhythm right, and taking your partner's pulse!)

You need: a partner, a bench or box 40cm high, a watch.

- Get your partner to step on and off the bench 25 times per minute for four minutes.
- 5 seconds after stopping, measure how long it takes your partner's pulse to do 30 beats.
- 60 seconds after stopping, do the same thing.
- 120 seconds after stopping, do the same thing.
- To work out your partner's stamina factor:
    1. Add up the three pulse counts.
    2. Divide the total into 12 000.
    Rating: 200 or less: good; 200–250: average; 250–300: weak.

6 How healthy are you?

- Use a height–weight chart on the worksheet to find out if others in your group are the right weight for their height.
- Do a survey of your group's other habits: exercise, smoking, diet. Write a report that lists the good and bad points you discover. Make recommendations for change if they are needed.

EXTRAS

1 Make a chart of all the activities you do in a day. Put them in order, with the most strenuous first.

2 Find out whether other members of your family are healthy. Make some recommendations about how they can improve their health.

3 Ask some fit people why they exercise and what they feel like afterwards.

7·7 *Exercise*

Sporting skills

To be good at any sport you need to have a range of skills. But each sport is different. Table-tennis players need quick reactions and good co-ordination. Shot putters need speed and strength.

Here are some comments by some people who have been at the top of their sport.

Sebastian Coe

To run fast you have to train the mind as well as the body. A lot of it is coordination. You cannot improve your basic speed; you can't alter your muscle composition. The important thing is to work on strengths and not weaknesses.

I've trained over the peaks from the age of 11 or 12. The weather in winter is so uncertain, it can be really cutting when the fog and ice close in. I've been out on occasions wearing three tracksuits and a waterproof. On some runs I've come back with my eyelashes frozen.

Chris Bonington

It was one of the hardest pitches I have ever done. After the first few moves there was no turning back. I balanced up from one rocky projection to another, soon realised it was even steeper than I thought, found myself thrust backwards out of balance. I knew that if I slipped I should almost certainly be killed.

Lucinda Green

You've got to read your horse like a book. You've got to know exactly what he is thinking and exactly how he's feeling. I think you've got to be totally in tune to be successful with a horse.

What skills do different sports need?

Here are some skills needed in sport:

strength	sharp thinking
speed	quick reactions
stamina	experience
suppleness	keeping calm
balance	intelligence

1 Which special skills do Lucinda Green, Chris Bonington and Seb Coe need for their sports?

● With some friends, discuss which skills are important in each of these sports:

weightlifting	ice skating
snooker	hockey
100m hurdles	cycling

● For each sport, make a list, with the most important skill first.

Kick-off!

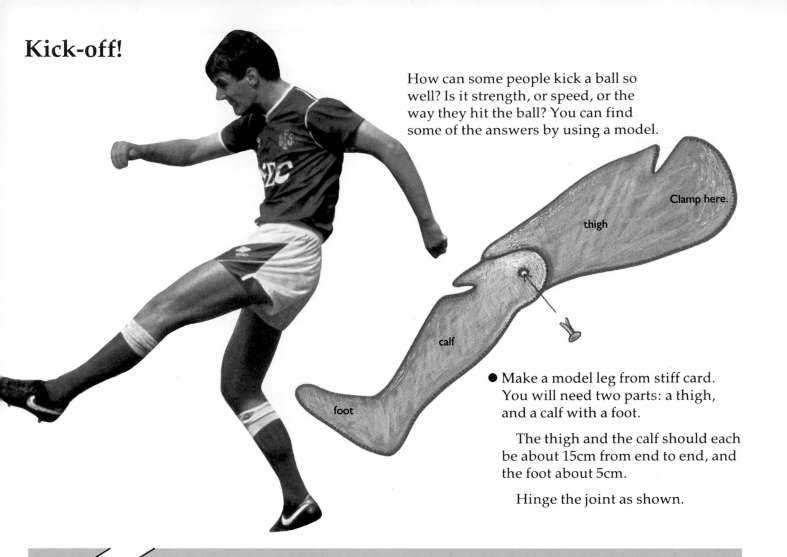

How can some people kick a ball so well? Is it strength, or speed, or the way they hit the ball? You can find some of the answers by using a model.

Clamp here.

thigh

calf

foot

● Make a model leg from stiff card. You will need two parts: a thigh, and a calf with a foot.

The thigh and the calf should each be about 15cm from end to end, and the foot about 5cm.

Hinge the joint as shown.

Investigating

Testing the model leg
● Fix the top of the thigh in a clamp so it cannot move. Then do three investigations:
● Make your leg kick a ball as far as possible. Use a Plasticine ball about 2cm across. Use an elastic band, fixed only to the leg or the clamp, as a 'muscle'.
● Find out if the position of the 'muscle' (elastic band) affects the result.

● Use a table-tennis ball or a squash ball. Find out how you need to change the leg to kick the ball as high as possible. You may need to make a new 'calf', with the foot at a different angle.
● Write up your results and your findings.

EXTRAS

1 Which sport do you think gives the best all-round exercise? Explain your choice.

2 Most sports people 'warm up' before exercise. What is warming up? Why do they do it?

3 Which of these statements do you think are true? Explain your answer in each case.
– Hockey players could play better with heavier sticks.
– Footballers could kick better with heavier boots.
– Golfers could hit better with heavier clubs.

On this page you will find a lot of different activities. They are all about accidents, illnesses and first aid. You will find most of the answers in the pages that follow. These pages contain information about:

accidents	heart disease
how diseases spread	cancer
fighting disease	first aid
smoking	

Communicating

Activities

1. What would you do?
(**a**) You are playing hockey when a friend gets a stick in her eye and starts bleeding badly.
(**b**) You are playing football when a friend is tackled, falls and cannot stand up.
(**c**) You find a two-year-old child with an open bottle of bleach beside her.
(**d**) Your mother spills boiling water on her arm and then collapses on the floor.
(**e**) Your younger brother is unconscious on the floor. He is holding an electric kettle connected to the mains.
(**f**) You disturb a nest of wasps and get badly stung.

2. What can you do to help someone who is ill in bed with a high temperature?

3. With your friends, make an anti-smoking or anti-alcohol or anti-sneezing poster.

4. Prepare a short talk or tape for your class about accidents. Choose one place where accidents may happen, like the kitchen or a place outdoors. Find out information about what goes wrong and when it goes wrong. Say what should be done to stop accidents in that place.

5. Make a map of the roads around your house or school. Mark on all the danger spots, and say why they are dangerous. Write a list of ideas which would make the area safer.

6. Find out about smallpox: what it is and how it has been controlled. You will need to use a library to do this.

7. Choose one disease (either from the rest of this unit, or one you can find out about). Make a pamphlet (to go in a doctor's surgery) about the disease. You should say what causes it, what it does to you and how it can be cured or prevented. What photos or drawings should go in the pamphlet?

8. Ask older people what illnesses were common before about 1960. Which ones are still common? Find out why some illnesses have nearly disappeared.

9. Design a poster that shows someone who has a high risk of heart disease, and someone who has a low risk.

10. Get permission to study the graves in a graveyard. Find out if people who lived long ago died at a younger age than modern people.

11. Most factories have to do a 'safety audit' every year. This means checking the entire factory for dangers and doing something about them.

Do a 'safety audit' of your house. Make a note of each possible danger. Suggest a way that it could be dealt with.

12. Write a story about this newspaper headline: 'Manned Mars probe returns with killer illness'.

EXTRAS

Do a survey to find out what illnesses each person in your class has had. Draw a chart to show your results clearly. Choose one of these:
– a pie chart.
– a bar chart.
– a line graph.

REFERENCE 1: Accidents

Where accidents happen

Every year, nearly 15 000 people in Britain die in
accidents. Over a quarter of these accidents
involve stairs or ladders.

Where accidents happen

Place	Deaths	Injuries
At work	850	500 000
On the road	6600	341 000
At home	6200	1 000 000

DANGER

Accidents at home

Fatal accidents in the home

This table shows how many people died in 1986
from accidents in their homes.

Cause of death	Age group					Total	
	0–4	5–14	15–44	45–64	65+		
Poisoning	4	8	276	153	110	551	(10%)
Falling	26	1	113	299	2828	3267	(59%)
Fire	73	40	101	139	394	747	(14%)
Suffocation	53	20	124	104	154	455	(8%)
Other causes	49	10	80	87	268	494	(9%)
Total	205	79	694	782	3754	5514	(100%)

Accidents on the road

This chart shows how many road accidents there are each year at different times
of the day.

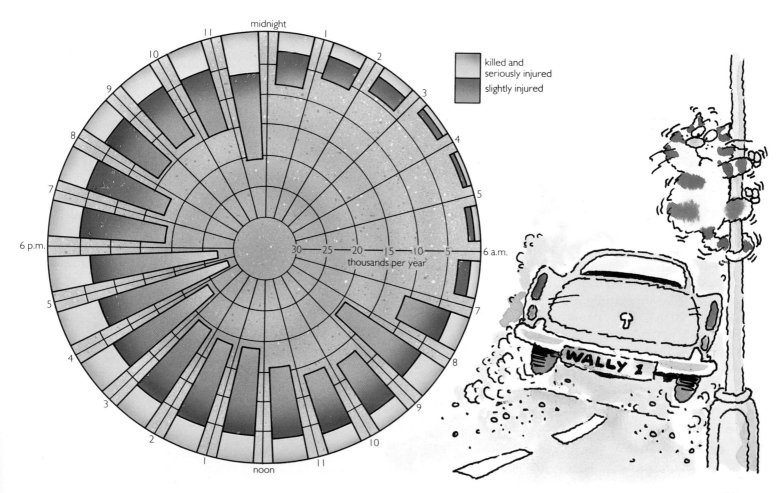

What is a disease?

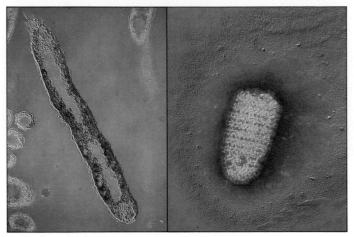

A cholera bacterium   *A virus particle*

You become ill when your body is infected by a virus or bacterium. These microbes reproduce inside your body, and make you ill. Often it is not the microbes themselves that causes the illness, but the poisons they make as they reproduce.

Most diseases have three stages:
1. Incubation: the microbes reproduce. You may not feel ill at all.
2. Sickness: the microbes take control and you feel ill. They do this because they can reproduce so fast.
3. Recovery: your body fights the disease. The microbes are killed and you get better.

How do diseases spread?

A person who has a disease is *infected*. Some diseases spread easily from one person to another. They are called *infectious* diseases. A quarter of all the deaths in the world each year are due to disease.

With some diseases, a person who is infected may spread them just by coughing or sneezing. Each time they do this, 20 000 drops of saliva are released. Each drop could be carrying a microbe that could infect someone else.

Other ways that infections can spread are by touching. These are called *contagious* diseases.

When a disease spreads very fast to a lot of people it is called an *epidemic*.

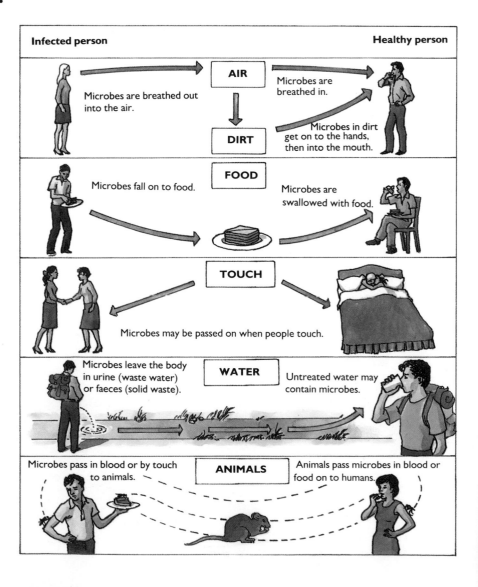

Some information on diseases

Disease	How it feels	What causes it	How long it lasts	How it is spread	How it can be prevented
Common cold	Sneezing, runny nose	Virus	3–4 days	Droplets in air	
Malaria	Weak, fever and shivering	Single cell (protozoon)	Can come and go during rest of life	Female mosquito	Anti-malarial medicines
Mumps	Painful, swollen jaw, temperature	Virus	3–4 days	Droplets in air	Immunisation
Measles	Rash, cough, runny eyes and nose, temperature	Virus	14–21 days	Droplets in air	Immunisation
AIDS	Many symptoms of many diseases	Virus	For ever	In blood and semen	No treatment yet available
Cholera	Sickness, diarrhoea, severe thirst and stomach cramps	Bacterium	1–5 days	Infected water	Water purification
Whooping cough	Painful, lasting cough	Virus	A few weeks to several months	Droplets in air	Immunisation
Diphtheria	Painful swelling of the throat and neck	Bacterium	3 weeks	Droplets in air	Immunisation
Chicken-pox	Skin rash – pock marks	Virus	A few days	Droplets in air	
Flu (influenza)	High temperature, weakness, aching	Virus	1–2 weeks	Droplets in air	Immunisation against epidemics only
Polio	Fever and paralysis	Virus	Paralysis may last for ever	Droplets in air, infected water	Immunisation

An epidemic riddle

There was a serious epidemic of cholera in London in 1848. Over 500 people died in ten days. Cholera is a very serious disease. First you get sickness and diarrhoea, then you get very thirsty, with bad stomach pains. Cholera victims usually die within two weeks of getting the illness.

In 1848 no one knew how diseases spread from one person to the next. A local doctor called John Snow talked to some of the sufferers before they died. He discovered that they all used the same water pump: 'I suspected some contamination of the water from the much-frequented street pump in Broad Street.'

Dr Snow took away the pump handle, and the cholera epidemic stopped immediately.

Cholera outbreaks happen now when people have to drink untreated water. It is one reason why severe flooding or drought can cause illness.

A COURT FOR KING CHOLERA.

Cells in the blood

Your blood contains white blood cells that help to fight disease. You will have over a thousand million of them.

There are different types of white cell. Some destroy microbes by surrounding them and then digesting them. Others make antibodies which break up microbes or make them easier for the white cells to attack. Other white cells remove the poisons that the microbes make when they reproduce.

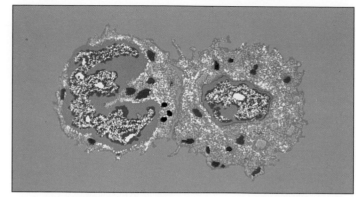

The white cell (on the left) is destroying a microbe.

Immunisation

You can build up resistance to a disease if you are immunised. Usually you are injected with a liquid that has dead microbes in. The white cells in your body make *antibodies* to get rid of the dead microbes. This may seem useless, but the antibodies stay after the microbes have gone.

If a living disease microbe gets into your body later, the antibodies to destroy it are already in your blood. They can destroy the microbe before it makes you ill.

Immunisation has reduced the problems caused by many diseases in the world. Diphtheria, a disease that used to kill many children, is no longer a serious problem in Britain, because babies are immunised.

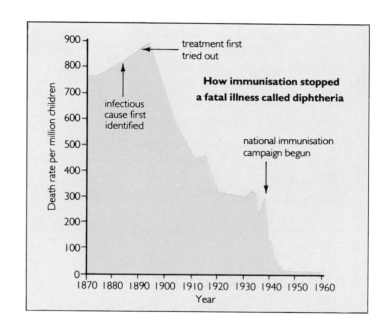

Medicines

Medicines do many jobs. Some help to fight disease by killing bacteria in your body. Antibiotics work in this way.

Some medicines do not fight disease, but make the disease less painful. Aspirin and paracetamol work in this way.

Some medicines try to make the body's own defences work better. Homoeopathic medicines are thought to help the body like this.

Antiseptics kill germs that may enter your body if you cut yourself. They can only be used on the outside of your body. If they get inside, they can damage healthy cells.

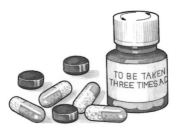

Cigarettes contain a drug. Once you start smoking, you find it hard to stop. Here is some information about the effects of smoking on your body.

Smoking and heart disease

How smoking affects the chances of getting heart illness

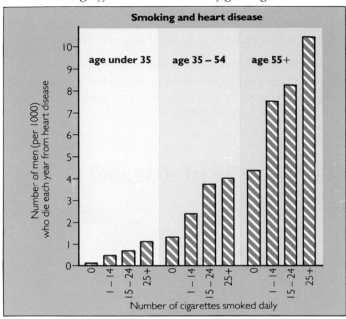

Smoking and cancer

How smoking affects the chances of getting cancer

Cigarettes smoked per day	Cancer risk factor
1–14	8 times normal
15–24	13 times normal
25 or more	25 times normal

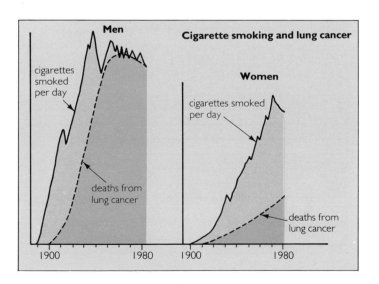

People's smoking habits

Smoking habits are changing.

	1972 (%)	1982 (%)
Men: have never smoked	25	32
used to smoke	23	30
do smoke	52	38
Women: have never smoked	49	51
used to smoke	10	16
do smoke	41	33

Do children smoke?

A survey was done to find out how many children smoked. Here are the results:

Age	12	13	14 (%)	15	16
Boys: have never smoked	92	80	66	60	45
used to smoke	4	10	9	14	14
do smoke	4	10	25	26	41
Girls: have never smoked	92	81	70	53	47
used to smoke	3	9	9	14	14
do smoke	5	10	21	33	39

Smoking and breathing

Every time that you breathe in, your lungs fill with air and lots of other things like dust and dirt. This photo shows a human bronchial tube. It carries air to and from the lungs. The tiny hairs, called cilia, help to move muck out of the lungs.

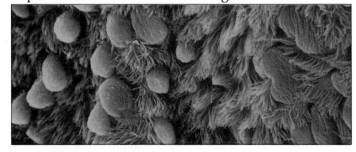

People who smoke are filling their lungs with extra muck. This damages the cleaning hairs and stops them working. The tiny air passages in the lungs get blocked, and the lungs cannot do their job properly. If a smoker gives up smoking, it could take many years for his or her lungs to work as well as they used to.

Heart attack!

'I was working too hard, I know I was. I tried to take it easy, but the phone kept ringing and I had to stay late to get the orders for the next day. If I didn't sort out the problems, who would?

We should have had a walking holiday last spring, but it was such a rush to get things ready at work that we couldn't go. In fact, I can't remember when I really relaxed before the attack.

I was sitting watching the news and having a drink to help me relax when I got this pain across my chest. Just like a vice crushing my chest. I tried to get up, but it got worse, and that's all I can remember.

I was one of the lucky ones. The doctor got to me in ten minutes. He told me later that during a heart attack the muscles of the heart are starved of oxygen. In a bad attack the heart can stop beating altogether, and you may die. In any case, the damaged muscles never recover completely.

Anyway, as you can see, I'm not smoking, and I'm not drinking much. I've lost some weight and I'm taking it easy. If the work isn't done by 5.30 p.m., then I just leave it. And I'm walking more to keep myself fit.'

What is a heart attack?

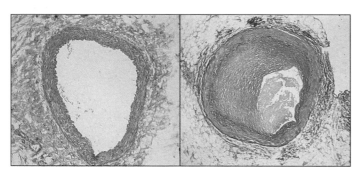

Left: A cross-section of a healthy artery. Blood flows down the clear space in the middle. Right: An artery which is narrow because of disease. The pale parts are the signs of a blood clot in the artery.

The coronary arteries supply blood to the heart muscle. As you get older, particularly if you do not exercise your heart and if you smoke, the arteries gradually get narrower.

If the arteries get badly blocked, oxygen may not reach the heart muscle. You then get pains in the chest, and you may get a heart attack. The heart can even stop beating altogether.

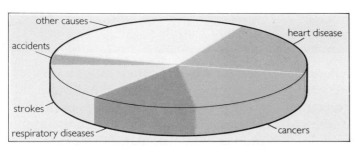

Heart disease is one of the major causes of death in Britain

Who gets heart disease?

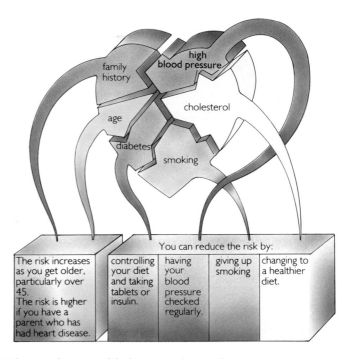

What makes you likely to get heart disease

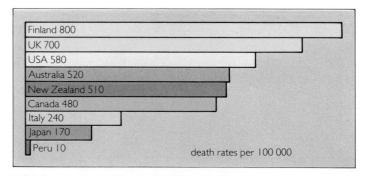

Which countries have most heart disease

REFERENCE 6: Cancer

What is cancer?

A cancer is a group of cells that grow in the body. They do not do a job for the body like the other cells. They just grow. As they grow, they use up the food, oxygen and space that other cells in the body need.

Sometimes these useless cells stop growing and stay in one place. Sometimes they go on growing, and spread to other parts of the body. If cells spread, they can be very dangerous and even deadly.

There are over two hundred types of cancer. Most cancers can be cured if they are found before they grow too big, or spread far. Because there are so many different types, there is no one sign that you have cancer. But it is always wise to see your doctor if you have a problem that does not get better quickly.

Scientists are not sure what causes cancer. They know that some substances, like nicotine from cigarettes and asbestos from old buildings, make it more likely that you will get cancer. They know that some types of people are more likely to get cancer than others. But they have not found out in most cancers why the cells go wrong.

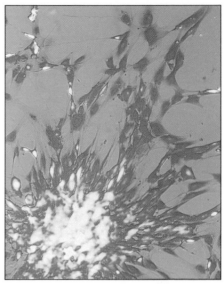

A cancer tumour. The smaller cells on the outside will spread around the body.

Who gets cancer?

Cancer can attack anyone. But there are things you can do to reduce your risk of getting it.

Number of deaths from lung cancer per million people under 65

	Male	Female
Smokers	300	100
Non-smokers	25	20

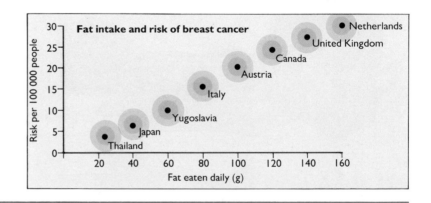

Cancer treatment

Some types of cancer can be cured nowadays. They can usually be stopped if they are found early. There are three main types of treatment.

Having an operation
The cancer cells are cut out from the body. This is called surgery. It is used if the cancer cells are in one place and can be removed without taking out too many healthy cells.

Radiotherapy
Rays are shone at the cancer cells to destroy them. Modern machines can pinpoint the cells so that few healthy cells are damaged.

Using drugs
Because cancer cells grow and reproduce fast, they are sensitive to some drugs. These drugs can kill the cancer cells without damaging the healthy cells. This is called chemotherapy.

Drugs are also used to reduce the pain that cancer may cause.

The discs on the patient's chest show where the rays are aimed.

REFERENCE 7: First aid

Imagine the scene: you are walking to a friend's house when a man cycles past you. He swerves to avoid a car that pulls out, and he crashes into a telephone box. He is bleeding and seems to be badly injured. What would you do first?

Before you read on, write down what you would do.

1. Get someone to telephone for an ambulance.

2. Do not move the man if he is unconscious, or if he has any pain in his back.

3. Is he breathing? Listen for breaths at the man's mouth. At the same time, look if his chest is moving (**A**). If he is not breathing, check that nothing is blocking his mouth (like false teeth) (**B**). Tilt his head back: this opens the airway to the lungs, and moves the tongue away (**C**). Now you can give him mouth-to-mouth ventilation (**D**, **E**).

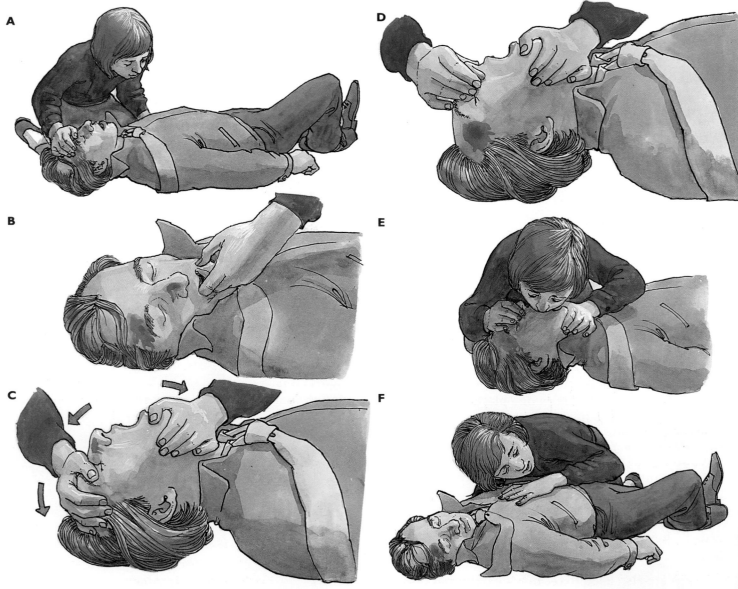

4. Is his heart beating? Mouth-to-mouth ventilation is no good if the person's blood is not flowing. After a few ventilations, check the man's heartbeat (**F**).

If there is any pulse (**G**), carry on with the ventilation. If there is no pulse, listen on his chest for a heartbeat (**H**). If the heart has stopped, press down on it *hard* (**I**). This pushes blood into the arteries. Do five slow pushes, down and up. Then give another mouth-to-mouth ventilation. Check the pulse again and repeat the chest presses if there is no pulse. Continue this sequence until help arrives.

5. Is the man bleeding? If there is a lot of blood, press a pad on the wound, or push the sides of a cut together. If possible, raise the injured part and support it.

6. If there may be a broken bone or back injury, do not move the man. Serious damage can be done by moving an injured person. Otherwise, put him in the recovery position. Keep him warm until help arrives. Do not give him anything to eat or drink.

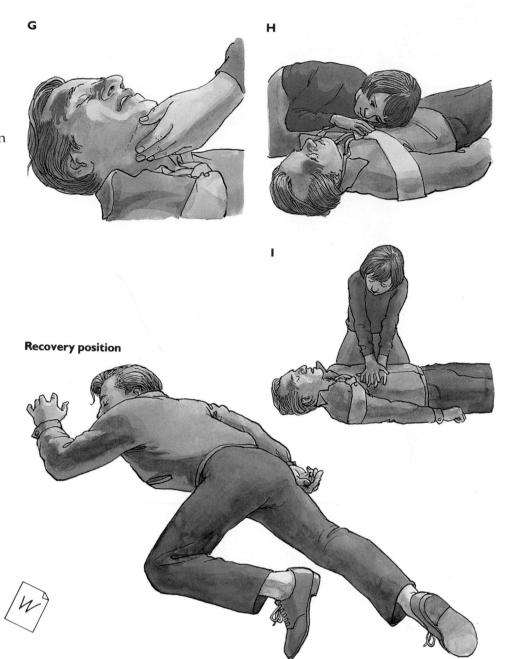

Recovery position

Some minor injuries

Bruises
Raise the injured part. Put cold water or ice in a plastic bag on the injury. Keep the rest of the person's body warm.

Burns
Cool the burn under cold water for at least ten minutes. Take away any clothing covering the burn. If the burn seems bad, get help. If the burn is not serious, cover it with a plain dressing. Do not use a plaster or cotton wool.

Cuts
Wash your hands. Wash any dirt or bits out of the cut with clean soap and water. Dry it, and put a dressing or plaster on. Bigger cuts may need stitching.

Fainting
If the person is conscious, get them to sit with their head between their knees. Loosen any tight clothing. If the person is unconscious, treat her or him like the person in the accident above.

Sprains
Get the person to lie down. Raise the injured part and support it. Put cold water or ice in a bag on the injury for at least ten minutes. Then bandage the injury. If there is a lot of pain or swelling, the person should have an X-ray.

You can learn a lot more about how to deal with injuries if you do a first-aid course.

8 ENERGY

8:1 What is energy?

All these pictures have something to do with energy. What do you think energy is?

● Write down one word that means the same to you as 'energy'.

1 Which word have most people in your class written down?

Using energy

● Collect pictures about energy from magazines and newspapers. Look for things that use energy, and how they get energy.

● Use your pictures to make a poster about energy.

How much energy?

● Which of these needs most energy to work? Write them down in order, starting with the one that you think needs the most.

● Which of these gives you most energy? Write them down in order, starting with the one that you think gives you the most.

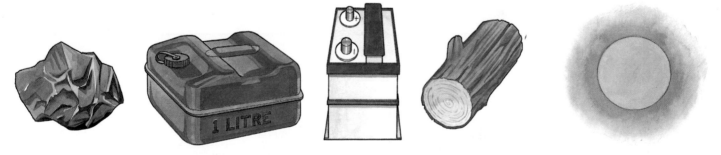

● Which of these contains the most energy? Which contains least? Put them in order.
● Discuss your lists with your friends. Try to make three lists you agree on.

EXTRAS

1 Make a list of five things that you do each day. Put them in order, starting with the one that you think needs most energy.

2 Make a list of five things at home that use energy. Put them in order, starting with the one that uses most.

3 A car battery and a litre of petrol are both energy stores. What other ways are there of storing energy?

8.2 Fuel

Mountain fuel

I went to the Lake District with my school last summer. One day we climbed a mountain. Before we left, our teacher made sure we had a big breakfast. Claire and I don't really like baked beans on toast, but we ate them.

We took a packed lunch: some peanut butties and a special mint sugar bar called Kendal Mint Cake. Our teacher, Mr Gibbs, carried some extra chocolate bars. "In case you lot run out of fuel," he said. He also had a small gas stove for heating water if we needed a hot drink.

We set off quite early. It was all uphill, and we were soon sweating. By lunchtime we were tired and dead hungry. After lunch we had to go up a steep rock called Jack's Rake. There was a huge drop on one side, and it was quite scary. Claire got stuck in one place, and Mr Gibbs had to rescue her.

When we got to the top, it was windy and cold. We put all our spare clothes on and had some of our Mint Cake. Mr Gibbs made us a hot drink beside a stream. Then we went down the path. Back at the Hostel we felt really hungry and tired.

● A fuel is a store of energy. Make a list of all the 'fuels' in the story.

1 How were the fuels used up in the story?
2 Why were the climbers 'really hungry and tired' at the end?

Motor fuel

Peugeot 205 XLD

SPECIFICATIONS	
Engine: cubic capacity	
Fuel consumption	1769cc
Constant driving 56mph (90km/h)	
Constant driving 75mph (120 km/h)	26 km/litre
Simulated urban driving	19 km/litre
	18 km/litre

A Peugeot will go about 26 kilometres on one litre of fuel. If you had to push a Peugeot 205 for 26 kilometres, it would take a lot of energy. But that is the same energy as there is in a litre of diesel fuel that the Peugeot uses.

Train fuel

The 'Royal Scot' was a train that used to run between London and Edinburgh. It took about 6 hours to do 630 kilometres. A locomotive such as the 'Leander' pulled the train.

Investigating

Comparing fuels

- Plan an investigation to find out whether diesel fuel or solid fuel gives out more heat. For safety you should use a special solid fuel instead of coal. It contains about the same amount of energy.

Warnings ⚠️

1. You cannot put a thermometer in the flame. The glass would break.
2. Diesel fuel is highly flammable.
3. These special solid fuels are poisonous.

- Ask your teacher to check your plan, then carry out your experiment.

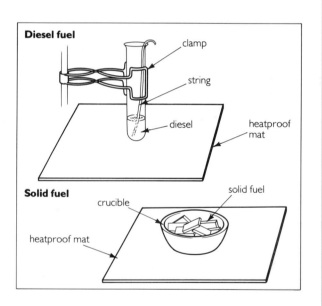

- Write a report on your experiment.
- Work out how long you think a whole litre of diesel would burn for.

3 Do you think a Peugeot 205 burns diesel at this rate? Explain your answer.

4 Do solid fuel and diesel fuel burn the same? Explain your answer.

- The 'Royal Scot' used about 7 tonnes of fuel to get from London to Edinburgh. Make an estimate (from your results) how much water this amount of fuel would boil.

EXTRAS

1 Find out how diesel fuel is different from petrol.

2 Why don't cars use coal as a fuel? Make a list of reasons.

3 Do a design for a car that *could* run on coal.

4 Which fuels do trains use nowadays? Which do you think is best? Why?

5 Write a short story of your own that uses the words 'fuel' and 'energy'.

8·3 Where do fuels come from?

Coal

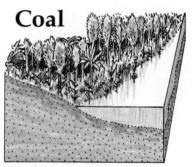

Plants and trees store energy from the sun as they grow.

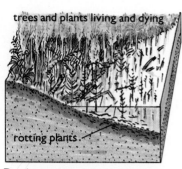

Dead animals and plants fall into swampy ground. They are covered by water. This stops air from getting to them, so they do not rot away.

A thick layer of dead vegetation forms. Over millions of years, this becomes coal.

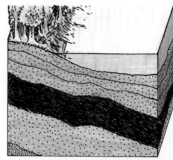

At the same time, layers of mud and other rocks are left above the coal.

Britain has many coal fields.

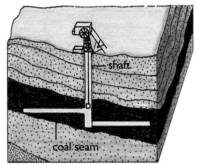

To reach the coal, miners dig shafts through the rocks to the coal seams. Miners cut tunnels as they take out the coal.

Oil and gas

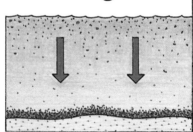

Tiny animals live in the sea. When they die, they fall into the mud at the bottom. The sea stops them from rotting away.

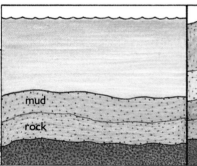

Over millions of years, many layers of mud form over the animals. Some of these layers become rock. The dead animals become oil and gas.

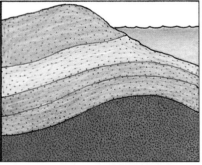

Movements in the Earth squash and fold the layers of rock. Oil and gas move up through the rock because they are lighter than rock. If there is a hard rock layer that will not let gas or oil out, the fuels get trapped.

There is oil and gas trapped between layers of rock under the North Sea.

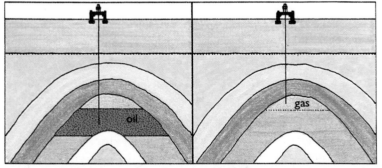

People use drilling rigs to pierce the rock layers and remove the fuels.

Making fuels easier to use

Oil, coal and gas straight from the ground are usually impure and messy to handle and use. They have to be changed into cleaner fuels.

Wood is also a good fuel, but it makes smoke when it burns. It is useful to make it into a cleaner fuel.

Oil

When oil comes from the ground it is a lumpy, thick, dirty liquid. No engine could use this as a fuel. The crude oil has to be cleaned and split up into useful parts first. This happens in an oil refinery.

An oil production platform.

A razorbill with its feathers covered in oil.

boiling point, like gas and petrol, go to the top of the column. Parts with higher boiling points, like diesel, condense before they reach the top. Liquids with very high boiling points, like bitumen, run down to the bottom of the tower.

The different parts are collected separately. They have to be refined even more before they can be sold.

Coal

Some coal, like anthracite, can be used straight from the ground. Poor-quality coal can be changed into coke by being heated away from the air.

At the same time, tar and gas are made. Tar is used on roads, and it can be turned into drugs, dyes, disinfectants and soaps. The gas can be used for heating, and is made into other chemicals.

The diagram shows you one way of improving coal as a fuel.

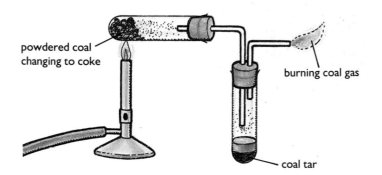

powdered coal changing to coke

burning coal gas

coal tar

Wood

In many countries, wood is a very important fuel. One problem with burning wood is that it smokes. This does not happen if the wood is made into charcoal. You can try this.

- Choose one of the fuels on this page. Design and make a display about the fuel. The display should be for pupils your age. It should be easily understood by people who know nothing about fuels. Make sure it is interesting and eye-catching!

Refining oil

fractionating tower

liquefied petroleum gas (LPG):heating

40°C

naphtha: petrol, solvents

175°C

kerosene: paraffin, jet fuel

250°C

gas oil: furnaces, diesel fuel

300°C

lubricating oil: lubrication, vaseline

400°C

400°C

heavy oil: candles, bitumen (roads)

crude oil

petroleum

The hot crude oil comes in to the fractionating column near the base. All the vapour rises up the column. The parts of the crude oil which have a low

EXTRAS

1. Why is wood used as a fuel in some countries? What problems are there in using wood as a fuel?

2. If you were building a new house, which of the fuels on this page would you use to heat it? Why?

3. Coal, gas and oil are all called *fossil* fuels. Why?

8·4 Which fuel should I use?

What things are important in a fuel? Here are some things you might look for:

– Is it easy to get or mine?
– Is it easy to light?
– Does it produce a lot of heat?
– Is it clean?
– Is it cheap?
– Can you transport it easily?
– Does it cause pollution?

● Plan tests to find the good and bad things about some plant fuels. Make sure your tests are fair. Get them checked and carry them out.

You should be able to use small pieces of: wood, coal, peat, charcoal, coke, coalite, paper. **Take care!** Some of these fuels can get very hot even when they still look quite cold.

● Write a report on what you found. You could include oil and gas in your report, but you cannot test them in the same way as the solid fuels. It would be dangerous.

Making fuels into electricity

Many fuels are made into electricity. Electricity is easy to transport and easy to use. The main problem with it is storage. You can only store very small amounts of electricity.

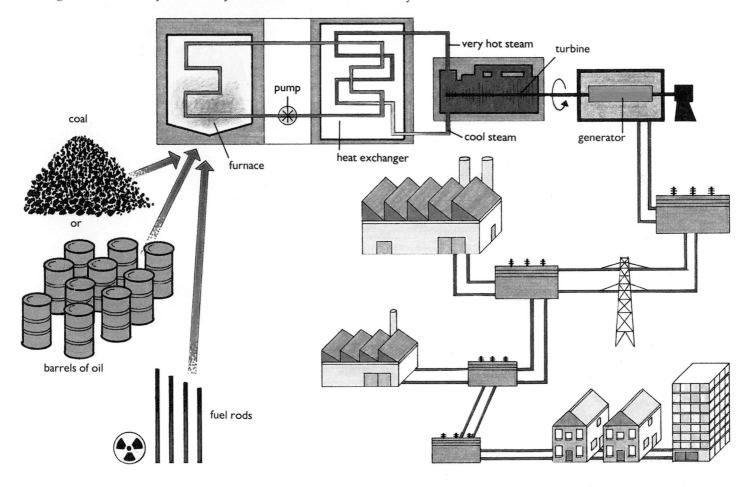

coal

or

barrels of oil

fuel rods

very hot steam
turbine
pump
cool steam
generator
furnace
heat exchanger

Communicating

- Do a page for a primary-school science book about electricity. Include information about how it is made, and its good and bad points.

- Do a flowchart to show how a fuel in the ground becomes the electricity for a computer in your school.
- Find out:
  (a) at what times of day most electricity is used.
  (b) what Economy 7 electricity is.
  (c) what the National Grid is.

EXTRAS

1 Petrol, potatoes and peat are all fuels.
(a) Think of three useful jobs that each fuel could do.
(b) Each of these fuels could help to keep you warm. Explain how you would use them to do this.

2 Make a magazine advertisement for a fuel. You have to persuade people to buy your fuel. Choose one of these: oil, wood, coal or gas.

3 Make a list of some fuels that are not mentioned on this page. Try to find out what they are made from and what they are used for.

4 Think of a way that you could use other fuels to do the jobs that electricity does in your home. For example, you could use wax (a candle) for lighting.

8·5 Running out of energy

Fuels are used up when they give up their energy. Fuels like wood can be replaced in a few years. Trees may be cut down and burnt, but new trees grow again in 20 or 30 years. Wood is a *renewable* fuel: it is replaced in less than 50 years. But even so, in some countries wood gets used up faster than it grows.

Coal, oil and gas took millions of years to become fuels. We use them up much faster than they can form. They are called *non-renewable* fuels. Scientists estimate that we will have used up these fuels quite soon:

Fuel	There will be almost none left in
Oil	35 years
Coal	250 years
Gas	50 years

▼This map shows where the fuel reserves in the world are:

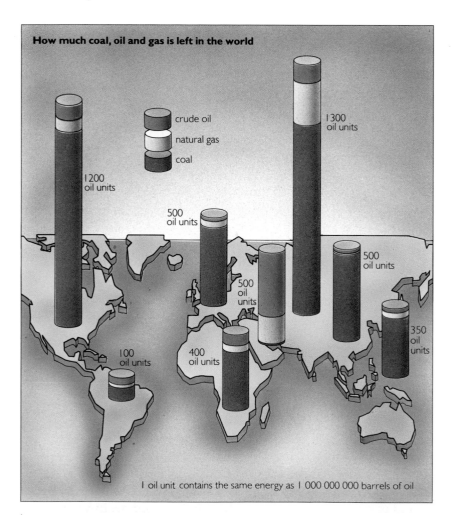

How much coal, oil and gas is left in the world

crude oil
natural gas
coal

1300 oil units
1200 oil units
500 oil units
500 oil units
500 oil units
350 oil units
100 oil units
400 oil units

1 oil unit contains the same energy as 1 000 000 000 barrels of oil

1. Which countries have the biggest reserves of (a) coal? (b) oil? (c) gas?
2. The map does not include reserves of trees as fuel. Why not? Where are trees likely to be an important fuel?
3. There is probably a lot more energy left in the ground than the map shows. Can you think of some reasons why?
4. Do you think we are likely to use more or less energy in the future? Explain your answer.
5. Your younger brother has read this page. He says that before he gets old there will be no cars, only bicycles. Is he right? What would you say to him?

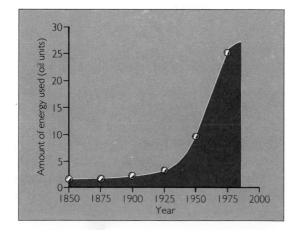

These estimates will only be right if we keep on using fuels as we are now. One extra problem is that we are actually using them faster and faster:

Making fuels go further

Everything that uses energy also wastes it. For example, a light bulb uses energy to make light. At the same time, it gets hot, which is a waste of energy. *Efficient* things use energy better and waste less.

Almost all our energy goes on our homes, transport and industry.

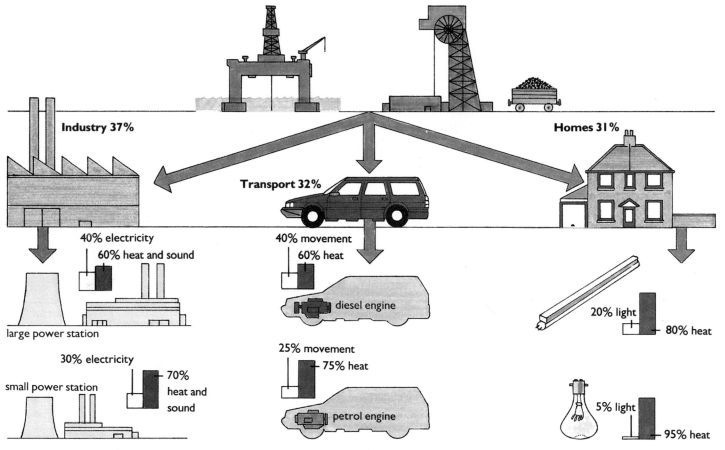

Industry 37%

40% electricity
60% heat and sound

large power station

30% electricity
70% heat and sound

small power station

Transport 32%

40% movement
60% heat

diesel engine

25% movement
75% heat

petrol engine

Homes 31%

20% light
80% heat

5% light
95% heat

● Do a pie chart that shows where most of our energy is used.

● Give some examples from this chart of energy being used more efficiently.

An average British family uses energy like this:

Heating the house	40%	Heating water	10%
Transport	25%	Food eaten	5%
Electrical goods	16%	Cooking	4%

● Do a display that shows how a family uses energy.

6 Where and how do you think you could save energy?

Cutting out waste

Does your school waste energy?
● Plan and carry out a survey of energy wastage in your school.
● Write a report for your headteacher with ideas for improvements.

EXTRAS

1 Do an energy wastage survey at home. Suggest to your parents that they should pay you a percentage of any savings!

2 Are you most efficient when you use energy quickly or slowly? Design and carry out an investigation with a bicycle. You can use ten complete turns

of the pedals. Does the bike go further if you pedal quickly or slowly?

3 Think of some ways of getting energy that will not run out.

8·6 Energy from the sun

Plants need the sun's energy to grow, to produce oxygen, and to make fruit.

All of your energy comes from plants in the first place. So does oxygen.

The sun also uses fuel to produce heat and light. The sun's fuel comes from the atoms it is made of. Scientists think that this fuel will run out in a few million years. Then the sun will cool down. What will happen to the Earth?

Food from the sun

Plants turn the sun's energy into fuels. One common fuel made by plants is starch. A potato is a good example of this. The fuel is made in the green leaves of the plant and is then carried to other parts of the plant.

● Plan an investigation to see if a geranium plant needs sunlight to make starch in its leaves. It will take a geranium several days to use up the starch in its leaves.

How to test leaves for starch ⚠ 🕶

● Put a piece of leaf in boiling water for 1 minute.

leaf
boiling water

● Turn out any flames, then get some meths.

● Put the leaf in a test-tube of hot meths till the leaf goes white. (**Take care:** fire risk.)

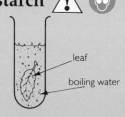

hot meths
very hot water

● Dry it on a paper towel.

paper towel

● Put iodine solution on the leaf: black = starch, brown = no starch.

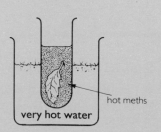

iodine solution

white tile

1 How will you be sure it is the sun that has made the starch?

Discuss your plan with your friends and your teacher, then carry it out.

Where does starch come from?

Plants make starch from carbon dioxide and water. The potato plant uses the sun's energy to join these chemicals together.

Here is an experiment that Mary and Richard did about carbon dioxide and starch. Read what Richard wrote, and then try the questions. You may be able to try their experiment yourself.

sunlight

carbon dioxide into leaves

water and minerals

Do plants need carbon dioxide?

The teacher told us to use bicarbonate indicator to test for carbon dioxide.

First, Mary tested the indicator by blowing slowly through some in a test tube. It started dark blue, went orange and then yellow as Mary blew.

Next we got two pieces of pondweed. We washed them with distilled water to make sure they were clean.

We made some bicarbonate indicator just orange by blowing very gently into it. Then we set up our experiment. We left all the tubes in bright sunlight for an hour. After one hour, we took the foil off tube 2 and drew the test tubes.

Before   aluminium foil
1   2   3

After
1   2   3

● What else does Richard need to say? Finish off his account.

2 Explain:
(a) why the indicator in tube 1 went blue.
(b) why the indicator in tube 2 went yellow.
(c) what the experiment tells you about plants.

3 Why was the pondweed in tube 2 kept in the dark?

4 Why was foil used on tube 2 instead of a black paper bag?

5 What was tube 3 for?

EXTRAS

Planning

1 Can a geranium plant make starch if it only gets light of one colour? Design an experiment to test some coloured light to see which colour is best.

2 Put some pondweed in a large syringe nearly full of pond water. Block the end up, and leave it in the light for a few days. Test any gas by blowing it over a glowing spill. Explain your results.

3 Bicarbonate indicator is one way of detecting carbon dioxide. Can you think of another? Why do you think bicarbonate indicator is better for plant experiments?

8·7 Energy chains

Producers and consumers

The grass makes starch from the sun. Grass is called a *producer*.

A cow eats the grass. It is called a *primary consumer*.

A human eats meat from the cow. He/she is called a *secondary consumer*.

Plants need the sun's energy to grow. All animals have to eat plants or other animals to live. With your friends, think of some other examples, then try these:

● Write down three other producers.
● Write down three other primary consumers.
● Write down three secondary consumers.
● Think of one animal that can be both a primary and a secondary consumer.

acorn blackbird cat fox
geranium plant greenfly
human ladybird lettuce
pig rabbit

● Make a chart that shows all the links between these living things. Draw all the producers on the left-hand side of your page. Spread them out if you can. Then draw an arrow from each producer to the animals that eat it. Then draw arrows from each animal to any other animals that eat it.

What happens when plants die?

This is a heap of dead plants. They rot away because tiny organisms called bacteria feed on them. These bacteria live in the soil and in the air.

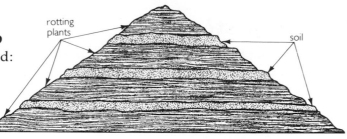
rotting plants
soil

Making a good compost heap

To make a compost heap you will need:
– some unwanted plants and grass
– a safe place outside for your heap
– a plastic cover for the heap

Instructions

Sprinkle ROTTO liberally over your compost heap when rain is expected. If your compost heap is covered, water the Rotto in. You should sprinkle ROTTO on every 10 cm depth of vegetation.

'ROTTO' compost accelerator is supposed to make compost rot faster. Look at the instructions on the packet.
● Do an investigation to find out if ROTTO really does work.
● Look at your heaps every day or two for a month. Gently look in the middle of each heap, but do not disturb it too much.
● Keep a diary of what the heap looks like.
● Look for small animals in the heap. Identify them if you can.

1 Why do you think you need to put some soil in the heap?
2 What do you think is in compost accelerator?
3 Why do you think it helps to cover the heap?

What happens when animals die?

Animals rot with the help of other animals. Flies lay eggs on rotting flesh, and the eggs hatch into maggots. The maggots eat their way into the damp, dark carcase.

Chemicals in the dead animal's cells are released by the maggots. These chemicals help to dissolve the tissues, and these are washed into the soil. A gas called ammonia is also released. This smells like a baby's wet nappy.

EXTRAS

1 Some farms in Britain have methane digesters. A methane digester collects the gas made from rotting manure, and uses it for cooking or heating. Why don't houses in Britain have them for cooking? Why do some families away from cities in Africa and India use methane digesters?

2 Food that is left out will rot. What can be done to stop this?

3 The Tollund Man in the photograph lived about 2000 years ago. His preserved body was found in a bog in Denmark. What do you think stopped him from rotting away completely?

8·8 Using energy

Which is cheapest?

Campers need a fuel that they can carry round with them. There are many different fuels and stoves to choose from. Which would you choose?

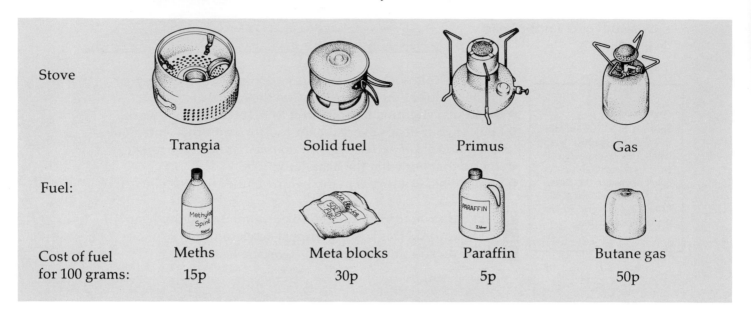

Stove	Trangia	Solid fuel	Primus	Gas
Fuel:	Meths	Meta blocks	Paraffin	Butane gas
Cost of fuel for 100 grams:	15p	30p	5p	50p

Planning

- Plan an experiment to find out which stove is cheapest to boil water with. If your school has these stoves, you may be able to test your plan.

- A meths stove takes about 5 minutes to boil enough water to make two cups of tea. It uses about 20 grams of meths to do this. Plan an experiment to find out if it is cheaper to use a Bunsen burner. (A Bunsen burner costs about 1p for 10 minutes.) Get your plan checked and carry it out.

How hot?

Normal thermometers cannot be used to measure flame temperatures. One way of comparing flames is to use a safety match. Hold the wooden end in tongs, and put the end that lights into the flame. The quicker the match lights, the hotter the flame.

- Plan an experiment to compare the temperatures of a yellow Bunsen flame, a roaring Bunsen flame, burning paper, a candle and a spill. Again, remember that you need to measure, not just look. Make sure that each one is tested in exactly the same way.

   If your teacher thinks you can do the experiment safely, she may let you try your plan out. **Warning:** take great care to follow your teacher's safety rules.

Is cost everything?

Cost is not the only important thing in choosing a camping stove.

Here is some more information:

Stove	Trangia	Solid fuel	Primus	Gas
Fuel	Meths	Meta blocks	Paraffin	Butane gas
Weight of stove	250g	100g	750g	400g
Is the fuel easy to light?	*****	***	*	****
Is the fuel clean?	****	*	**	*****
Is the fuel easy to buy?	***	*	***	***
Is the stove easy to use?	****	***	*	****

(The more stars, the better or cleaner the fuel is.)

1. Which stove would you take with you if you were:
  (**a**) hiking alone in the mountains? Why?
  (**b**) cycling with a friend along the coast? Why?
  (**c**) camping with your family in France? Why?
  (**d**) on a Sunday outing in the car? Why?
  (**e**) living alone in a caravan? Why?

How easy is it to light?

If you have to make a fire in the mountains, you need a fuel that will light very easily.

● Plan an experiment to find out how easy it is to light some different fuels. Try to find a way of measuring this – using your eyes alone is not very scientific.

You may be able to carry out your plan. If so, take great care. Get your teacher's approval first. Make sure you know how to put fires out before you start!

A forest fire. Some fuels, such as dry wood, are very easy to light, and people must be careful not to start fires by accident.

EXTRAS

1 Draw a flowchart to show how you would light a campfire with only newspaper, matches and wood.

2 Do a safety poster for children who have to use camping stoves.

3 Which camping stove would you use for a camping holiday if the price of all the fuels doubled?

Insulating houses

We spend a lot of money heating the air in our homes. It can be very expensive if the heat gets out and warms the air outside as well. Insulation is used to stop the heat from escaping.

This house has not been insulated. The owners pay £800 a year for heating. The picture shows you where the money goes.

● Draw a picture of the house, then decide how you could insulate each part. Put labels on your drawing that show what you would do.

Here is the same house after it has been insulated.

1 What is the total heating bill now?

All these places have been insulated: windows, floor, doors, walls, roof.
● Put them in order of energy saved.
● Write the amount of money saved beside each one.

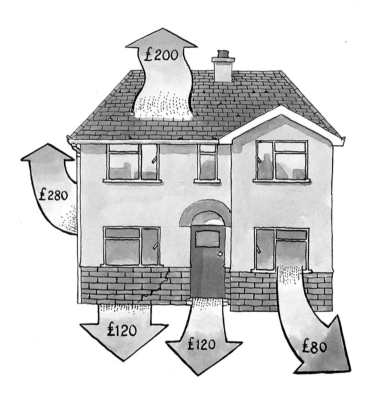

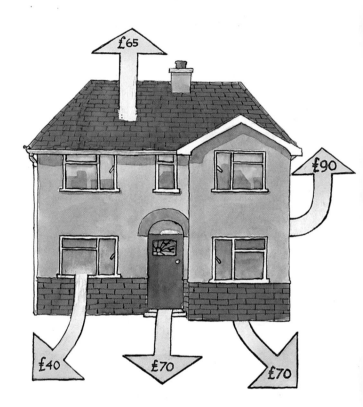

Roof insulation

● Design an investigation to find out how good three types of insulation are:
  – 5cm layers of ceramic fibre insulation
  – 10cm layers of ceramic fibre insulation
  – vermiculite
● Get your plan checked and carry it out.
● Write a report on your investigation.

Insulating your school

● How much heat could be saved in your laboratory? Use these figures to make an estimate of the energy wasted:

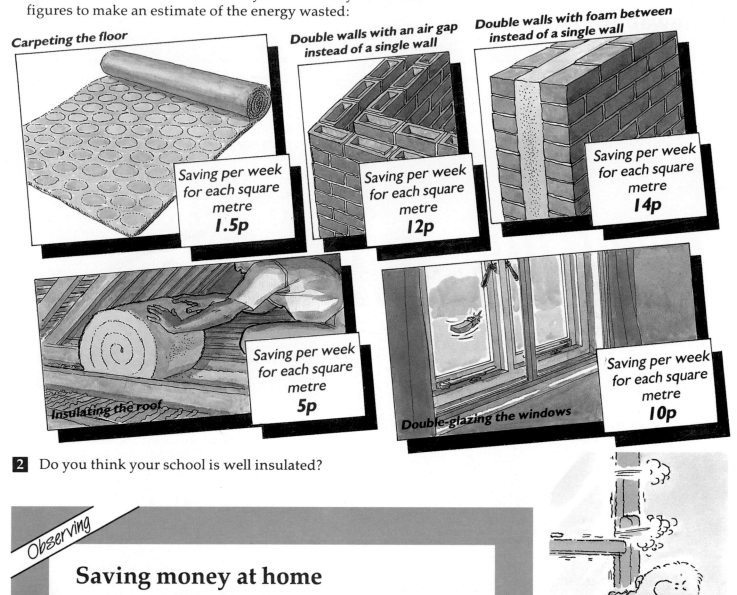

Carpeting the floor

Saving per week for each square metre **1.5p**

Double walls with an air gap instead of a single wall

Saving per week for each square metre **12p**

Double walls with foam between instead of a single wall

Saving per week for each square metre **14p**

Insulating the roof

Saving per week for each square metre **5p**

Double-glazing the windows

Saving per week for each square metre **10p**

2 Do you think your school is well insulated?

Observing

Saving money at home

● Go round your house or flat and write a report on how well insulated it is.
● Use the figures above to work out how much your parents could save each year by insulating your home better.
● If your home is not well insulated, find out why.

EXTRAS

1 In some countries near the Equator, the temperature can vary between 30°C in the day and 0°C, or less, at night. What problems would you have if you lived in a house there? How would you design your house to cope with both heat and cold? (Hint: look at some African house and hut designs for ideas.)

2 Collect information about energy and insulation from newspapers, magazines, local DIY shops and supermarkets. Make a poster that gives ideas on energy saving.

Renewable energy sources

Some energy sources cost nothing. But it is often difficult to get this energy in a useful form.

1 Water moving downhill can be used to generate electricity. This is the Cruachan Dam and power station in Scotland.

2 The change in water level when the tide comes in and goes out is used to make electricity in France.

3 The sun is a good source of energy, but it is hard to use it. The water in these houses is heated by solar panels.

4 In some places, the wind is a good source of energy. This generator in Wales is unusual: it spins horizontally on top of its tower.

5 There is heat underground that can be used to heat water. Many houses in Reykjavik in Iceland are heated like this.

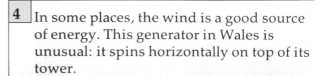
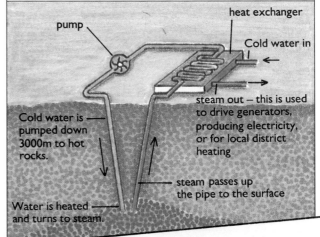

heat exchanger

pump

Cold water in

Cold water is pumped down 3000m to hot rocks.

steam out – this is used to drive generators, producing electricity, or for local district heating

steam passes up the pipe to the surface

Water is heated and turns to steam.

24/10/99 <u>Energy for ever?</u>

Description	Energy source	How it works	Would it work near you?	Problems
Hydro-electric power	Water	Water runs down-hill and drives a generator		

● Draw a table in your book:　　　　● Fill in the table. The first one has been started for you.

A solar heater

You and your friends have to get 10cm³ of water as hot as possible in 30 minutes using only the sun's energy. You can use the following materials:
– thick polythene bags
– scissors
– black and white paper or card
– tape
– a boiling tube
– plastic tubing
– a thermometer

You really need a sunny day to do this experiment. You could try using a bright light instead of the sun, but it will not work so well.

Before you start, look at the design of a solar water heater. You will not need a pump, or a hot water tank, but the design of the panel may give you some ideas.

- Plan what you will do.
- Decide what you will measure, and how you will measure it.
- Get your plan checked and carry it out.

- When you have finished, do a group report on your work. This should include:
  – your design
  – your results
  – things you could improve.

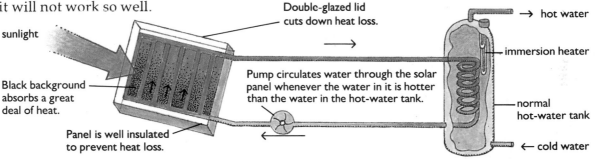

sunlight

Double-glazed lid cuts down heat loss.

hot water

immersion heater

Pump circulates water through the solar panel whenever the water in it is hotter than the water in the hot-water tank.

Black background absorbs a great deal of heat.

normal hot-water tank

Panel is well insulated to prevent heat loss.

cold water

EXTRAS

1 The sun's energy can be used to make electricity with solar cells. You may have a solar powered watch or calculator. This car does not use petrol; it uses the sun's energy.
(a) What equipment will the car need to change the sun's energy into movement?
(b) What problems are there in using this type of energy?
(c) Where else are solar cells used?

2 Household rubbish is a good energy source. Make a list of the things that you throw away that could produce heat. Why do you think there are not many 'household rubbish energy generators'?

3 We use more energy at some times of the year, and less at others. This graph shows you how.
(a) When do we use most energy? Why?

Across Australia – by sun!

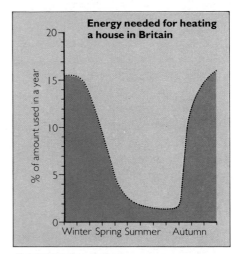

Energy needed for heating a house in Britain

% of amount used in a year

Winter Spring Summer Autumn

(b) Which of the energy sources on page 50 would give most energy when we need it? Which would not?

Nuclear energy

What is nuclear energy?

The sun produces energy from the hydrogen atoms it is made of. Nuclear power stations use the energy stored in uranium atoms. Atoms are very small. About ten million uranium atoms would fit across a pin-head. The energy is stored in the centre of the atom, the nucleus.

A uranium atom gives out energy when its nucleus splits up.

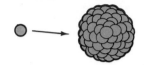

One neutron causes...

one uranium atom to split...

making it give off heat and radiation...

plus **three** more neutrons...

which will cause **three** more uranium atoms to split...

which will give off more energy, and nine neutrons, which will cause a chain reaction

Inside a nuclear power station: the machine is removing a used uranium fuel rod.

Nuclear energy is hard to control. If too many uranium atoms split at the same time, there is a nuclear explosion. To prevent this, a special reactor is used. The reactor controls the rate at which the atoms split. Even so, a lot of energy is produced, and the rods get very hot. Eventually the uranium fuel is used up.

This is how most British nuclear reactors work.

Nuclear power stations produce almost a quarter of Britain's electricity. Although they cost a lot to build, they are not very expensive to run. But there are two big problems.

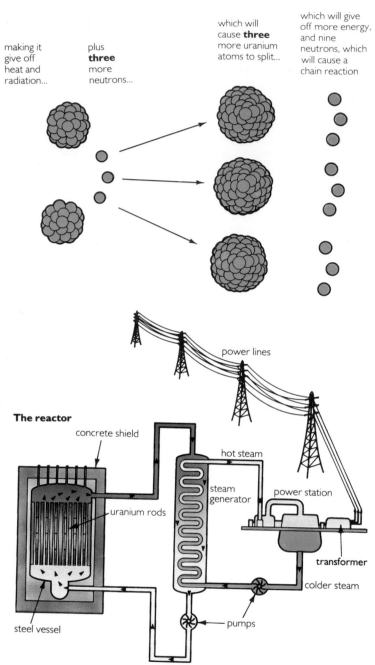

power lines

The reactor

concrete shield

hot steam

steam generator

power station

uranium rods

transformer

colder steam

steel vessel

pumps

First, uranium supplies are being used up. Eventually uranium will run out just like oil and gas will. Scientists are trying to develop other types of reactor that do not use uranium as the fuel.

Second is the problem of nuclear waste. One uranium fuel rod contains the same amount of energy as 150 tonnes of coal. But when the rod is used up, it does not leave ash that can be cleaned away. A used rod contains very dangerous radioactive chemicals. These have to be removed and stored until they are safe.

Is nuclear energy a good thing?

● What do you think about nuclear power? Make two lists. Put all the good things about nuclear power in one list, and all the bad things in the other.

The Sizewell A nuclear power station in Suffolk.

Communicating

Five-minute special

You and your friends are reporters for a local radio station. You are famous for giving accurate and interesting reports. They only last about five minutes, and come on in breaks in pop music. The reports are called: 'What do you think about . . .'

The government wants to build a nuclear power station 10 kilometres from your school.

● With your friends, make a script for the programme 'What do you think about the new power station?'
● Record the finished script onto a cassette tape. Your script should:
(**a**) give the facts about nuclear power
(**b**) put all sides of the case
(**c**) make it interesting (if it's not, the listeners will turn off)
(**d**) involve *all* your team.

EXTRAS

1 The sun's energy comes from *fusion* reactions. In a fusion reaction, small atoms are joined together to make larger ones. When they join, they give out energy.

Scientists are keen to make a fusion reactor. It would be powerful, and would have no radioactive waste. But there are some big, unsolved problems.

The atoms that are going to be joined have to be very hot: about 100 million Celsius. At this temperature, the hot atoms are hard to keep in one place. Finally, the energy has to be removed from the reactor.

Use your imagination. Do a sketch for a fusion reactor that overcomes these problems. Label the parts.

2 A nuclear power station is going to be built near you. Imagine that you are either an unemployed labourer or a farmer. Write a letter to your local newspaper saying why you want, or do not want, the station to be built.

Joe's problem

'It's not easy running a café like this. I get rushed off my feet half the day, and I get real aggro from customers if I don't serve them fast.

A new pizza house has just opened over the road. They seem to be able to make and sell food and drink much cheaper than I can. I don't know how they do it, but my customers know which is best for them.

Then there's the bills. Gas, electricity, rates, they all make a huge hole in my profits. I wish I could find a good way to improve things.'

Café Consultants Inc.

You are management advisers called Café Consultants. Joe has asked you for advice. Your job is to take a look at his problems, carry out tests, then to offer advice. Joe has prepared some questions for you, and your boss has put her ideas in as well.

```
Q1   Can I cut my gas and electricity bills?
```

Here are some photos taken in the café by one of your team.

- Look carefully at your photos.
- Write a brief report for Joe on things he might do to save money on gas and electricity.

> **Q2   What should I charge for tea?**

Your boss says you must investigate this.

- Design an investigation to find out how cheaply you can make a cup of tea with an electric kettle.

  Here are some prices:

  Milk: 5p/100cm^3
  Tea: 1p/bag
  Water: free
  Sugar: 5p/100g
  Electricity for 3kW kettle: 3p for 10 mins

- Get your plan checked and carry out your investigation. Make sure that you put enough water in the kettle to cover the element.
- Find out:
  – what a cup of tea costs if you half-fill the kettle with water.
  – what a cup of tea costs if you fill the kettle up to the maximum mark.
  – how much each cup costs if you make several cups of tea at the same time.
- Write a report on your results for Joe.
- Draw a bar like this next to each result. The bar shows the total cost of *one* cup of tea.
      Each centimetre is 1p.
      Red is the cost of the electricity.
      Brown is the cost of the tea.
      Blue is the cost of the milk.
      Green is the cost of the sugar.

Here is part of the menu from the pizza house opposite Joe's Café:

PIZZAS		BEVERAGES	
Margherita	£1·20	Tea (per cup)	25p
Italiano	£1·35	Tea (per pot)	40p
Romano	£2·10	Coffee (per cup)	40p
Mozzarella	£1·70	Milk (glass)	25p
Special	£1·65	Cola (glass)	30p

EXTRAS		SWEETS	
French fries	40p	Ice Cream (portion)	60p
Mushrooms	30p	Apple pie	60p
Side Salad	60p	Trifle	65p

- Add some more advice to your report for Joe. Tell him what you think he should charge for tea, and explain your reasons.

> **Q3   Could I make my own electricity?**

Joe's Café is in a small seaside town in Wales.

- Produce a short report telling Joe:
  – how he might make his own electricity
  – what equipment he would need to do it
  – whether you think it is possible.

| Electricity 6p | Tea 6p | Milk 3½p | Sugar 3½p |

EXTRAS

1 Are some kettles cheaper to run than others? Do a plan for an experiment to compare the cost of different designs of kettle. Be careful to say what you will measure, what you will alter and what you will keep the same.

2 Plan an investigation that would tell you if a gas stove or an electric stove or a microwave is cheapest for boiling water.

3 Look carefully at a thermos flask. Do a labelled drawing of it. If you can, find out how it works. How could thermos flasks help Joe to save money?

9 SENSES
9·1 Using your senses

How do you know where you are?

● Close your eyes and ask yourself how you know where you are.

● Now close your eyes and put your hands over your ears as well. How do you know where you are now?

It is almost impossible to stop all your detectors working. Each detector is a special cell. It sends signals to your brain throughout your life.

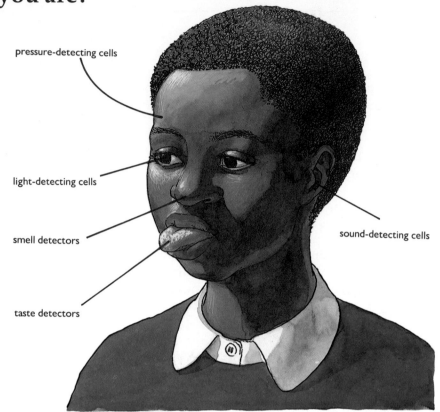

pressure-detecting cells

light-detecting cells

smell detectors

taste detectors

sound-detecting cells

Making sense

Our senses can detect many different things.

● Each activity here involves your senses. For each one you have to work out:
  – how many ways you can find to detect what is happening
  – which sense (or senses) you use.

Only taste things that your teacher says you can. ⚠️

● If you cannot detect anything, try to find a way of detecting it.
● Make a table for your results:

1 What is the difference between the blocks?

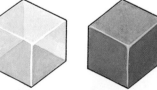
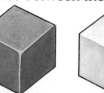
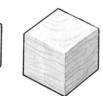

2 What is the difference between these crisps?

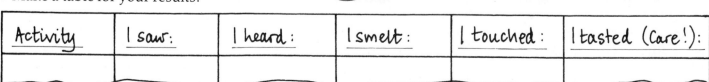

Activity	I saw:	I heard:	I smelt:	I touched:	I tasted (Care!):

3 What is the difference between the tubes?

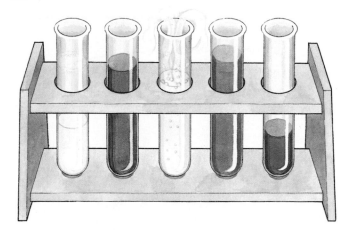

4 What is the difference between the papers?

5 What is the difference between the boxes?

Things you cannot sense

Sometimes your senses are not very good on their own.

● Can your senses detect any of these things? If not, think of a way of helping them.

1. The force that comes from a magnet.

2. The energy that comes from a battery.

3. The energy in a radioactive substance.

4. The energy in TV or radio waves.

EXTRAS

1 How are your senses different when you are under water at the swimming baths? Which senses work better? Which are worse? Which do not work?

2 Human senses cannot detect microwaves. Think of as many ways as possible of telling that a microwave oven is working.

3 One way of making static electricity is by rubbing plastic objects on material. Find out if your body can detect static electricity. If it can, which senses do you use? If not, how can you tell there is static near you?

9·2 Looking at light

Sight is one of your most important senses. Your eyes work because of the way light travels, and the way that lenses can change it. Your first task is to find out how light travels.

A shadow theatre

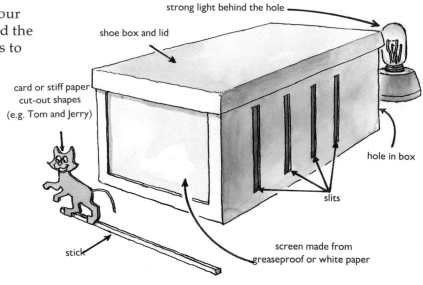

strong light behind the hole

shoe box and lid

card or stiff paper cut-out shapes (e.g. Tom and Jerry)

hole in box

slits

stick

screen made from greaseproof or white paper

- Make a shadow theatre from an old box:
- Test your theatre to make sure that the shadows are clear. They must be on the screen.
- Then use it to do these three investigations:

1 What happens to the shadow if you move your cut-outs further from the light?
- Make some measurements that prove your answer. (Hint: Measure the distance from the light to the cut-out, then measure the size of the shadow it makes. With several different distances you could make a graph.)

2 How can you make the shadows as clear as possible?
 – Is it best to have a small light hole or a large one?
 – Is it best to have the cut-outs near or far from the light?
 – Is it best to have a small or a large bulb?

3 Can you use your cut-outs to prove that light travels in straight lines? (Hint: Use a ruler to find out if the light hole, the top of the cut-out and the top of its shadow are in a line. Try it for several cut-out positions.)

Communicating

- Write up all your work. Try to write a very good description.
- Use sketches to show what you tried.
- Put any measurements down in tables.
- Write a few lines that make clear what you learnt in each investigation.

Light work

It is very important that people work in good lighting.
- Look carefully at these photos and decide which office has better lighting. Make a list of reasons – there are several.

Cheap photos

Cameras work in the same way as your eyes. But taking photos costs money.

Did you know that, with care, you can take photos with a camera that costs almost nothing? First you have to make a pinhole camera and find out how it works.

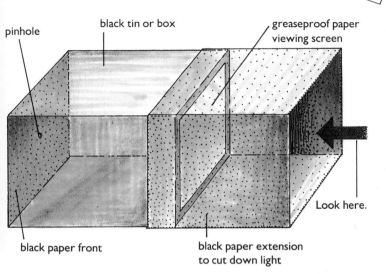

This photo was taken by a pinhole camera. The paper was this way round in the camera.

This is what the pinhole camera was photographing.

- Put a viewing screen of greaseproof paper in a pinhole camera where the film should be.
- Look at some bright objects like a light bulb or a window frame. What are they like?

- Do some sketches of what you see.
- With your friends, work out an explanation.
- Now you may be able to use your camera to take a real photo.
- Replace the screen with black card. You will need to fix the photographic paper inside this card in a darkened room.
- Take your picture outside in daylight. Allow about 5 seconds in sunlight for the exposure.

4 How is the pinhole photo different from the real scene?
5 Try to explain why the pinhole photo is like it is.
6 Look at a normal camera. What features does it have that make it better than a pinhole camera?

EXTRAS

Observing

1 Look at some different coloured things at night under a street lamp. What happens to the colours? Make a note of what you notice. Try the same thing in a different-coloured street light if you can. Make a note of what happens this time. Can you see any pattern in the results that might explain them?

2 Take a careful look at a newspaper photograph. What is it made of? How does it show different shades of grey? Try the same with a magazine colour photo – you may need to use a magnifier.

3 Look at the lighting in your home. Are any rooms poorly lit when they shouldn't be? How could you improve them?

4 Design a pinhole camera that would take pictures more easily than the one on this page.

9·3 Bending and reflecting light

Light travels straight as long as it does not hit anything. If it hits a lens or a mirror, then it changes direction. This can have some strange effects.

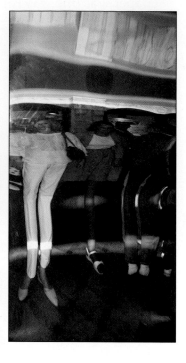

- Shine your beam of light on as many of these objects as you can. Observe each one carefully. Try different angles and directions.
  – mirrors (plane/concave/convex)
  – lenses (e.g. glasses)
  – small clear tank with water in
  – milk bottle with water in
  – glass block
  – polythene sheet
  – Perspex block
  – test tube with water in
  – prism

1 Which of these objects change the direction of the beam of light?
2 Which reflect it?
3 Which just bend it?

- Choose one of the objects you looked at. Do careful sketches to show the path of a light ray into, through and away from it.

Bending light

- Use a battery and a bulb to make a beam of light. Make the beam as narrow as you can by putting a shade with a slit in round the bulb.

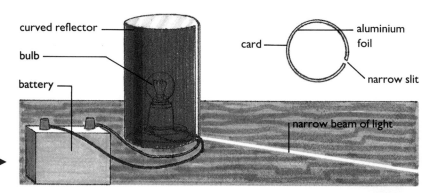

curved reflector · bulb · battery · card · aluminium foil · narrow slit · narrow beam of light

Investigating lenses and mirrors

There are two basic types of lens:

convex 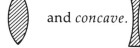 and *concave*.

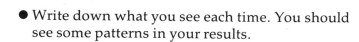

- Find out what happens to light that travels through lenses of different shapes. Test the lens close to your eye and at arm's length.
- Draw each lens that you use.
- For each lens, find out:
  – if the image you see is smaller or larger than the real thing,
  – if the image is the right way up or upside-down.
  (The image is what you see after the light has been through the lens.)

- Write down what you see each time. You should see some patterns in your results.

4 How do convex lenses differ from concave ones?

5 How do thin lenses differ from thick ones?

- Try a similar investigation with some different-shaped mirrors.

Using lenses

- Find out what types of lens are used to make a microscope.
- Use two lenses to make your own microscope.

- Practise using a proper microscope to look at a piece of cloth or a hair.
- When you can do it well, write or draw a set of instructions for someone who has never used a microscope before. The instructions should make it clear how to see a very small object clearly.
- Try your instructions out on a friend. Improve them, if necessary, after the trial.

- Use lenses to make one of these instruments:

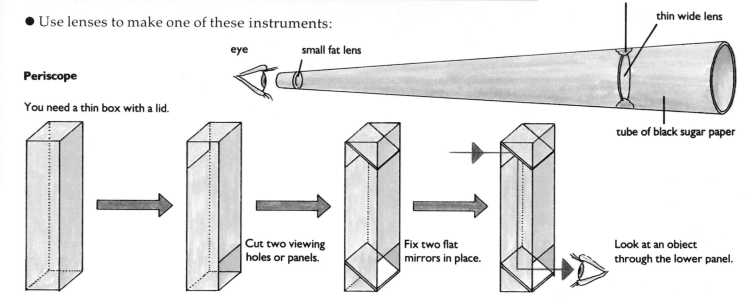

Telescope

Blu-tack

thin wide lens

eye   small fat lens

tube of black sugar paper

Periscope

You need a thin box with a lid.

Cut two viewing holes or panels.

Fix two flat mirrors in place.

Look at an object through the lower panel.

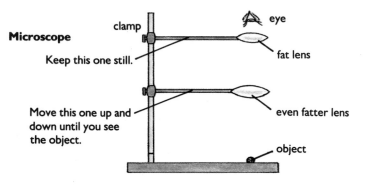

Microscope

clamp

Keep this one still.

eye

fat lens

Move this one up and down until you see the object.

even fatter lens

object

- Use card to make mounts for your instrument.
- Test the instrument to find out how it changes what you are looking at:

6 Is the image the same size as the real object? If not, how much bigger or smaller is it?

7 Is the image the same way round?

8 Is it the same way up?

9 Is the image distorted at all? (Distorted means not like the real thing.)

EXTRAS

1 Make a list of things in your house that use mirrors or lenses.

2 Design a periscope to look over high things or round corners. Can you find a way of altering your design so that the periscope can look in different directions without the person using it having to turn round?

Observing

3 (a) Put a penny in a large bowl or bath of water. Try to touch it. What do you notice?

(b) Stand a pencil in a glass of water. Draw a side view of it. What do you notice? Try to explain what you have seen.

9·4 Seeing things

Eyes

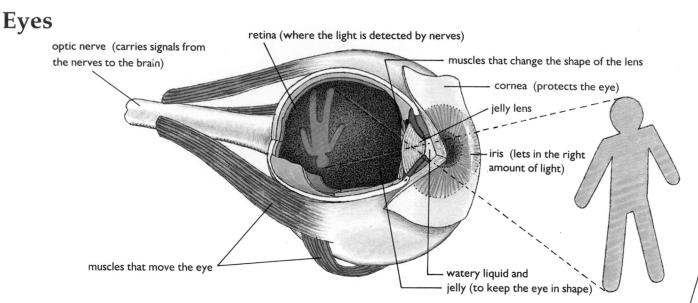

optic nerve (carries signals from the nerves to the brain)

retina (where the light is detected by nerves)

muscles that change the shape of the lens

cornea (protects the eye)

jelly lens

iris (lets in the right amount of light)

muscles that move the eye

watery liquid and jelly (to keep the eye in shape)

How good are your eyes?

Investigating

Far vision

- Plan and carry out an investigation to find out the answer to this question:

  How far away can I read this book?
- Test yourself and your friends. If you wear glasses, then keep them on. (You could try the same thing without your glasses if you have time.) Is the distance the same for each person?
- Now try the same investigation with some different-sized print. Try at least five different sizes.

- Write up your investigation. Take care to say how you made sure it was a fair test.
- Put your results on a graph like this one:

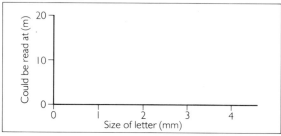

- Use your graph to predict how big the letters on a car number plate should be (a car number plate needs to be visible from at least 25 metres).
- Predict how big the letters on a motorway road sign should be. They need to be visible for at least two seconds to a driver going at 25 metres per second (60mph).
- Test your predictions on your friends.

Near vision

- Carry out a second investigation. Find out how near to your eyes you can read this page. Take care not to strain your eyes. Try different-sized print as before.

- Write up your investigation.

1 What differences can you find between near and far vision?

2 Can you explain them?

Seeing double

Why do most animals have two eyes?

In some animals, both eyes look the same way. In other animals they look sideways from the head.

3 What are the advantages of having eyes that look sideways?

Why aren't our eyes like that? Try catching a ball with one hand and you will soon see one important reason. Two eyes allow your brain to estimate *distance*. Each eye produces a slightly different view of the thing you are looking at. Your brain stores these views, does some instant calculations, and tells you if the object is close by or far away. This all happens without you even thinking about it!

Using two eyes like this is called *stereo* vision. It makes objects look solid like a model instead of flat like a drawing.

EXTRAS

Planning

1 (a) Who is better at reading things that are far away: older or younger people? Plan an investigation to see how your far vision compares with some adults you know.

(b) Try your plan out at home. Try to produce a graph that shows how the distance at which you can read this page varies with age.

2 Look carefully at a friend's eye in dim and bright light. What do you see? Which part of his or her eye is involved? Explain what is happening.

3 Which parts of your eye do the same jobs as the parts of the camera on worksheet 9.2C? Make a list of each part of a camera. Next to it, write down the part of the eye that does the same job.

4 Your eyes help you to estimate distance. If you look at something near, your eyes point inwards. To see a distant object, your eyes point ahead.

Use this idea to make a device that will measure distances. Find out how accurate it is.

Near object   Distant object

9·5 Hearing things

How does sound travel?

- Hold a blown-up balloon in your finger-tips. It will be a vibration detector. Hold it near some different sounds and you should feel it vibrate.
- Find out if it is *volume* (the loudness of the sound) or *pitch* (how high or low the sound is) that makes the balloon vibrate most.

Sound travels by shaking the air and sending waves through it. The waves spread out like ripples in a pond. You hear sounds when the air in your ear shakes and makes your ear-drum vibrate.

- Do a flow diagram that shows what happens when a sound reaches your ear.

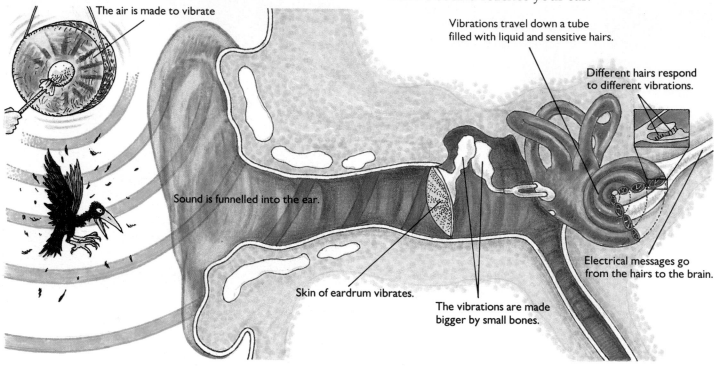

The air is made to vibrate

Sound is funnelled into the ear.

Skin of eardrum vibrates.

The vibrations are made bigger by small bones.

Vibrations travel down a tube filled with liquid and sensitive hairs.

Different hairs respond to different vibrations.

Electrical messages go from the hairs to the brain.

How fast does sound travel?

If something happens about 100 metres from you, you can often *see* it before you *hear* it. When a race starts over 100 metres from you, you see the smoke from the gun before you hear the gun. This happens because light travels much faster than sound:

1 About how long does it take sound to travel 300 metres?

2 How long for light to do the same thing?

- Think of a way to make your own measurement of the speed of sound.

Speed of light:
300 000 000 metres/second

Speed of sound:
330 metres/second

The light from the star Vega takes 26 years to reach the Earth.

Concorde can travel at over twice the speed of sound.

A sound detector

Sounds are difficult to detect. One method is to use a microphone to make the sound into an electrical signal. The signal can be changed into a trace by an *oscilloscope*. The height of the trace is a measure of the amount of noise (volume). The number of waves on the screen is a measure of how high the note is (pitch).

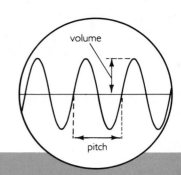

Planning

- Plan how you could use a microphone and an oscilloscope to find out how well sound travels in some different materials. You could use metals, wood, glass, water, plastic, materials, compressed paper.

- Think carefully about what you need to keep the same in each test:

– The same noise each time? Can you make a 'standard noise'?
– The same amount of material?
– The same detector?
How will you stop the sound travelling through the air to the detector?

You may be able to carry out your plan with your teacher.

Earthquakes

Earthquakes happen where the plates of rock that make up the Earth's crust meet. They send sound waves through the Earth that can be detected many thousands of miles away. An earthquake detector is called a *seismometer*.

You can make a model seismometer with a large screwdriver.
- Push the whole of the metal end of the screwdriver into the soil.
- Ask a friend to thump the ground away from the screwdriver whilst you listen on the screwdriver handle.

Earthquakes can cause enormous damage. In 1985, the earthquake in Mexico City killed 4000 people and destroyed hundreds of buildings.

3 How far away can you hear the thumps?

4 Does the sound travel better in the air or the soil?

EXTRAS

1 Do children hear better than adults? Find a quiet sound that you can just hear 1 metre away. Find out how far away other adults and children can hear the sound.

2 If you wait for a train at a station and listen carefully, you can often hear it a long time before you see it. Can you suggest why?

3 In cowboy films, Indians sometimes put their ear to the ground and listen. Why? Why is this better than sitting on a horse and listening?

Musical instruments

All musical instruments make the air vibrate when you play them. The strings on a string instrument are fixed to a box, and they make the air in the box vibrate.

When you blow a brass or woodwind instrument, the air inside the tubes of the instrument vibrates. When you hit a drum or cymbal, it sends vibrations into the air.

● Make and test some of these simple instruments.
● With each one, find out how to get high and low notes.
  – a stretched rubber band
  – a ruler over the edge of a desk
  – water in a milk bottle (tap or blow the bottle)
  – a comb and tissue paper
  – long and short pieces of metal
  – a tight string
  – a straw

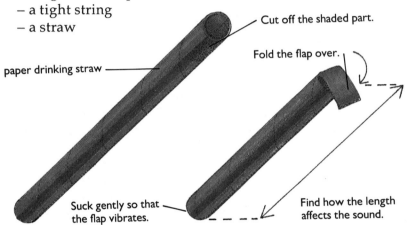

paper drinking straw

Cut off the shaded part.

Fold the flap over.

Suck gently so that the flap vibrates.

Find how the length affects the sound.

Investigating

● Use one of the simple ideas to make a musical instrument that can play at least five notes. You may need to use several bottles or strings to get all five notes.

It may help you to look at a real instrument that uses the same idea. You could try a violin or a harp of elastic bands, an organ of test-tubes, a xylophone of metal bits, or a whistle.

● Use your instrument to play the first three bars of 'Jingle Bells'. Can you play the rest?

● Write a report on your instrument. Say how it was made, how well it worked, and how it could be improved.

Sound patterns

All sounds have their own pattern. A tuning fork makes this pattern on an oscilloscope:

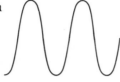

The taller the trace, the louder the note.

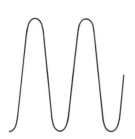

The more waves, the higher the note.

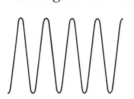

Here are the traces of three brass instruments playing the same note:

1 Which of these traces is the loudest?

2 How can you tell from the traces that each instrument is playing the same note?

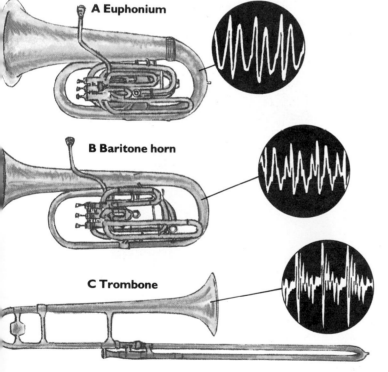

A Euphonium

B Baritone horn

C Trombone

3 Why do you think each instrument plays the same note? (It is something to do with the instrument itself.)

● Do a sketch of the trace you might get from a trombone playing a higher note.

● Do a sketch of the trace you might get from a euphonium playing the same note, but louder.

Painful sounds

Painful sounds can be a problem! ⚠

● Find out the best way to make ear protectors to keep sound out. You could cut and glue a basic muffler out of a plastic washing-up liquid bottle or make one from papier mâché. Then find out what is best to put inside it.

● Find out the best type of sound insulation for a noisy factory. You can make a model noisy factory from a tin can with a few coins or marbles in. Shaking or rolling the can will make a good racket. You have to find the best materials(s) to insulate the can with.

4 Which group in your class has got the best solution to these two problems? How will you decide?

EXTRAS

1 Which sounds are most annoying? Make a list of sounds that really annoy you (if you can, make a tape of the sounds). Get your parents and friends to put the sounds in order of nuisance.

2 Find a way of making the sound from a plucked elastic band as loud as possible. String instruments may give you some ideas.

Tasting

  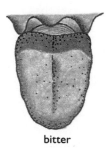

sour   sweet   salt   bitter

- Find out which areas of your tongue can taste each of these four tastes:
  - salt (salt solution)
  - sweet (sugar solution)
  - sour (lemon juice)
  - bitter (tonic water)

It is not usually safe to taste or eat anything in a science laboratory. You can only do it for this investigation if you use sterile equipment.

- Decide:
  - how you will make sure it is a fair test.
  - how you will know if all tongues are the same.
  - how you will record your results.
- Carry out the investigation carefully and hygienically.
- Write up your results.

Planning

Tasting tea

Some people say they can taste if a cup of tea has had the milk in before or after the tea.
- Plan an experiment to find out if most people can tell. Think of a way to tell if they are guessing.

Tasting crisps

All crisps taste the same when they are first made. Flavour is sprayed on to them later. Can your friends tell what flavour a crisp is without seeing the packet?
- Plan and carry out an investigation.
- Write a letter to the crisp makers about your results, with some advice about their flavours.

- Choose two flavours of crisp that are quite different. What is the smallest amount of crisp you need to taste to be sure which is which?
- Plan and carry out an investigation.

1 How can you be sure that each piece that you test has the same amount of the flavour on it?

Smelling

Smells are tiny particles in the air that your nose can detect. Each smell is a particular chemical. The smell sensors in your nose are sensitive to different chemicals, but many chemicals do not affect them at all. Animals are often more sensitive to smells than we are.

Some dogs are trained to sniff out drugs or explosives. They can smell the slightest trace of a drug on a person, in a car or on a ship.

Female gypsy moths give out a special scent when they are ready to mate. Male gypsy moths can smell the scent over ten kilometres away.

Even humans can improve their sense of smell. Skilled wine tasters can often tell the age and type of a wine just from its smell or 'bouquet'.

How sensitive are you to smells? ⚠️

Smelling salts are made from ammonia. The stronger the ammonia solution, the easier it is to smell.

● Start with a weak solution of ammonia that you can smell. Find out the weakest solution of ammonia that your partner can just smell. How will you stop him or her from guessing?

2 Are you as good at smelling as your partner is?

● Make a chart of the results for the whole class.

3 Is everyone's sense of smell the same?
4 Are girls more sensitive to smells than boys are?
5 Are the results the same if you use vinegar instead of ammonia?

● Find out if you can tell apart the four types of solutions you had to taste using just smell. You may need to make up some stronger solutions.

6 Which types of smell are you most sensitive to?

EXTRAS

1 Why does having a cold make it hard to smell and taste things?

2 Plan and carry out an investigation to find out the smallest amount of sugar you need to put in a cup of water to be able to taste it. Does it depend on the amount of sugar in your diet? Does it depend on what you have just eaten?

3 Can you tell crisps of different flavours apart using just smell?

9·8 Touch

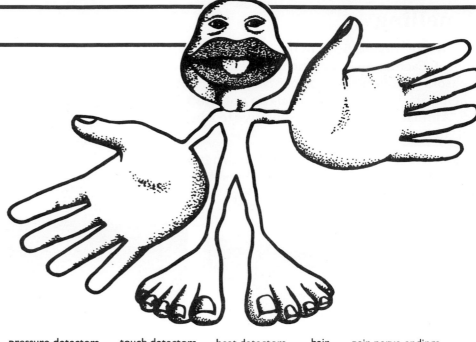

Sensors in the body

In this drawing the size of each part depends on how sensitive it is: the more sensors, the larger the part.

1 Which parts of the body are most sensitive? Why?
2 Which are least sensitive? Why?

There are three main types of detector in your skin. They detect touch, pressure and temperature.

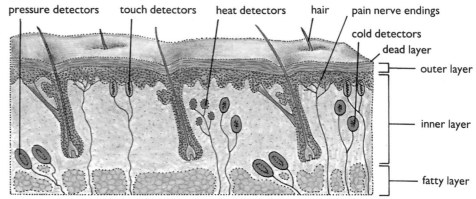

pressure detectors   touch detectors   heat detectors   hair   pain nerve endings
cold detectors
dead layer
outer layer
inner layer
fatty layer

Touch detectors

These are usually close to hairs. The slightest touch on a hair makes the sensor send a message through the nerves to the brain.

Pressure detectors

Other detectors which are deeper in your skin sense pressure. They help you to sort out heavier things from lighter things.

Temperature detectors

Temperature detectors detect either heat or cold. They are particularly common in your finger tips and in your lips.

Testing the sensors

● Find out the smallest piece of paper that your partner can detect when it is dropped onto the back of his or her hand.

● Find out which parts of your hand and arm are most sensitive to touch.

● Use your pressure detectors to sort some different objects into weight order. Find out the smallest difference in weight that your sensors can detect.

● Use your sensors to sort five beakers of water at different temperatures into order. Use a thermometer to check your results.

● Find out what happens if you do it again after keeping one hand in very cold water for a minute. Then try it after keeping the hand in very hot water, but be careful not to scald yourself.

Imitating touch

Human touch is very sensitive. You can pick up an egg easily without breaking it. It is much harder for a robot to do this.

● Design an arm to pick up an egg or a table-tennis ball without crushing it. The arm should be at least 30cm long and controlled from the end. It should be able to pick up the egg, carry it safely, and put it down again. The ideas here may help you.

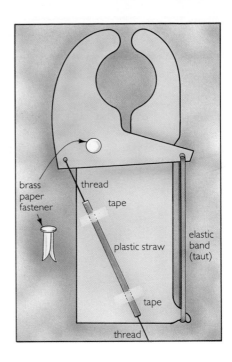

brass paper fastener — thread — tape — plastic straw — elastic band (taut) — tape — thread

Skin

Your skin is big. It weighs the same as a large bottle of lemonade, and covers an area as big as a dining table. It is waterproof and fairly disease-proof too. Touch sensors and sweat glands are part of it.

Skin colour depends on a chemical called melanin. The difference between people with black skin and people with white skin is that black skin contains more melanin. Ultra-violet light (from bright sunshine) can make white skin go darker.

Skin damage

Mary was badly burned in a house fire. Doctors knew it would take too long for live skin to spread over the burn from the edges. So they decided to move some skin from her leg to her face to stop scars from forming.

With a special fine razor they took a piece of live skin 25cm long by 12cm wide from her leg. This was stretched over the burned area and stitched. Within three days it was growing on Mary's face.

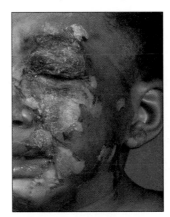

Skin grafts like this nearly always work unless they get infected. The patient has to have a good diet with lots of protein and energy food to help them to recover.

EXTRAS

1 Which sensors and senses would you use for these jobs?
(a) Finding a box of matches in the dark.
(b) Telling if a cake is burning.
(c) Picking up a freshly boiled egg.
(d) Reading Braille if you are blind.
(e) Playing a computer game.

2 Design, and make if possible, a model switch from card. It should switch from on to off or off to on with a gentle touch. The switch shown should give you an idea.

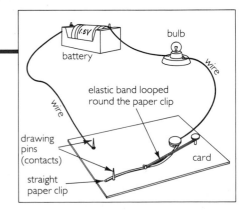

battery — bulb — wire — elastic band looped round the paper clip — drawing pins (contacts) — straight paper clip — card

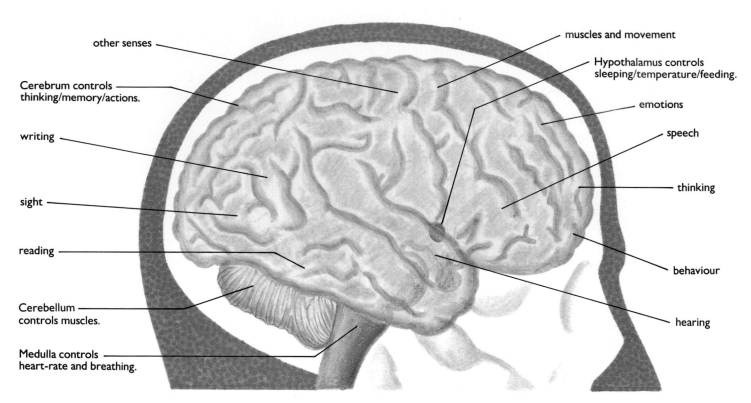

other senses

Cerebrum controls thinking/memory/actions.

writing

sight

reading

Cerebellum controls muscles.

Medulla controls heart-rate and breathing.

muscles and movement

Hypothalamus controls sleeping/temperature/feeding.

emotions

speech

thinking

behaviour

hearing

Every sensor in your body sends messages to the brain. The messages travel as electrical signals in your nerves. The brain sorts all this information. Each area of the brain deals with different senses.

The brain also deals with other sensors that you are not usually aware of. It checks your breathing, heart-rate, body temperature, chemicals in your blood and many other things. All this information is used by your brain to send messages back through your nerves to muscles and body organs.

Learning and remembering

IT'S NOT MUCH GOOD HAVING A BRAIN THE SIZE OF A SMALL PLANET IF YOU DON'T USE IT.

There is space in your brain to remember everything you have ever done. Even with all this filling your head, only about 1/100th of the brain's power is being used. Some people think that the brain records *everything* that you do – but that you cannot remember things because you cannot get them back.

A long time ago
Long-term memory is for things that happened some time ago.

● How many of these things can you write down?
(a) The names of the teachers you have had since starting at primary school.
(b) The names of the children in your first class in junior school.
(c) Your friends' phone numbers.
(d) A map that shows your route to school, or from your house to the local shops or town.
● Check your answers with your friends.

1 Do some people have better memories than others?

A short time ago

Short-term memory is used for things that happened in the last few minutes. The party game where you have to repeat and add to a shopping list needs a good short-term memory.

● Try the game. The first person can start with 'I went to the shops and I bought some sausages.' The next person repeats this, and adds something of their own. If you make a mistake of any sort, you are out.

2 What is the largest list that anyone can remember?

● Try the same game, but use only numbers. The first person chooses a number between 0 and 9. The second person repeats this, and adds a number.

3 Is it easier to remember numbers or objects?

Improving memory

Lots of things help you to learn well:
– You need to be comfortable and quiet.
– You need to learn actively (e.g. by making notes, not just listening).
– You need to use what you have learnt.
– You need to link the new information to what you know already.

● Look at these two graphs:

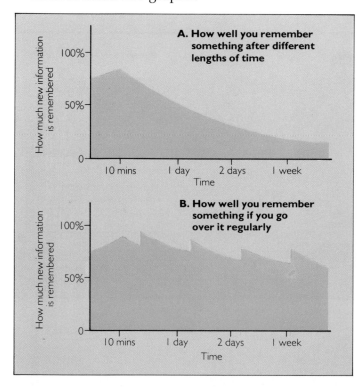

A. How well you remember something after different lengths of time

B. How well you remember something if you go over it regularly

4 How much new information is forgotten straight away?
5 About how much new learning goes into short-term memory?
6 About how much new learning stays in long-term memory?
7 Going over or reviewing new learning improves long-term memory. How much is learned at each review?
8 Write down a list of things that would help you to remember some new information.

EXTRAS

1 Teach yourself to write your name with the hand you do not normally use. Can you still do it some days later?

2(a) This is a learning challenge. Mix up two packs of cards. Time yourself to see how long it takes you to sort them into separate packs, with each suit arranged in order in each pack.
(b) Now find out if you have learnt from doing it. Plan the best way of doing the job again.

Carry out your plan and time yourself. Have you improved?
(c) Find out if two people working together can do it twice as fast as one person.

9·10 Communicating

Communication is the way we get information from one person to another.

- You have to get a message to your parents, telling them that you will be late home. Think of all the ways you might be able to communicate the message.
- Write down each method and note down the good and bad things about each one.
- Design and make a communication system that uses bulbs and wires. You have to send messages to a group 5 metres away. Agree on a code, and send these messages:
  - someone's name
  - someone's birthday
  - a simple drawing.

1 From your experiment, which things are easiest to communicate? Which things are hardest?

Shrinking the world

Switch on the television. What's on? Not *more* live sport from . . . These days it could be from anywhere in the world. Modern television uses satellites to send sound and pictures all over the Earth, and from the moon and planets to Earth. But how is this done?

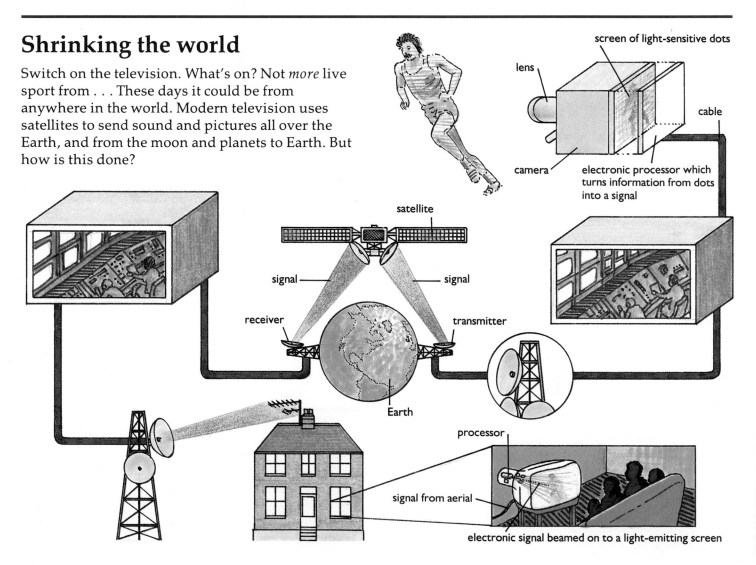

screen of light-sensitive dots

lens

camera

cable

electronic processor which turns information from dots into a signal

satellite

signal

signal

receiver

transmitter

Earth

processor

signal from aerial

electronic signal beamed on to a light-emitting screen

Getting the message across

- Without talking to anyone, write down what you think is happening in these photos.
- Then note down why you think this is happening.
- Compare notes with your friends. Do you all think the same?

2 What would these photos mean to someone from a small village in India?

- Cut out some adverts from old magazines and newspapers.
- Cover up any writing on the adverts.
- Find out if your friends can say what each advert is for.

3 How do advertisers get their message across?

Images

Logos are used to create an image of an organisation. Pictograms are used to give a message without words. Look at these:

4 What image does each of these give you?

Communicating

- With your friends try to design a logo or pictogram for:
  - your group
  - a fire exit
  - your school

EXTRAS

1 Watch the faces and hands of two people talking to each other. What do we communicate with as well as our voices?

2 Design a logo for your family. See if they understand what its message is!

3 Look at this communication system which was first used in 1837. How do you think it worked? How many characters could be sent with this system?

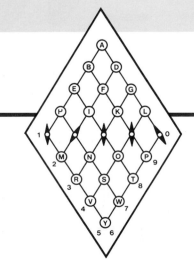

Lost senses

Touch, sight, hearing and speech are vital to us, but we take them for granted.

- Imagine that you had to do without each sense in turn. Think what the problems would be.
- With your friends, make a display to show how life would change for you if you did not have some or all of your senses.

Try these activities:
- Do up your shoelaces when you are blindfolded.
- Tell a friend an urgent message without using speech or writing.
- Walk from one classroom to the toilet, and back, when you are blindfolded. (Get a friend to help you.)
- Understand an urgent message from a friend without using hearing or writing.

- Imagine that a deaf person is coming to your school for a day. What problems would they have? What could you do to solve some of these problems?
- Imagine that you are blind and you spend a day at your school. Write a story about what it is like and what happens.

Helen Keller was deaf, dumb and blind from early childhood. Much later she did learn to speak, and could 'hear' words by touching the speaker's face and throat. Despite her handicaps, Helen Keller obtained university degrees and became a successful writer and lecturer.

Communicating with signs

Below are three 'sign systems' that do not use speech.

- Find out which of these systems is best for sending a short message quickly.

1 What could each of the sign systems be used for?

2 Sign language also has more complicated two-handed signs. What do you think the extra signs are for?

- Make up some signs suitable for: TV, bicycle, cold, angry.

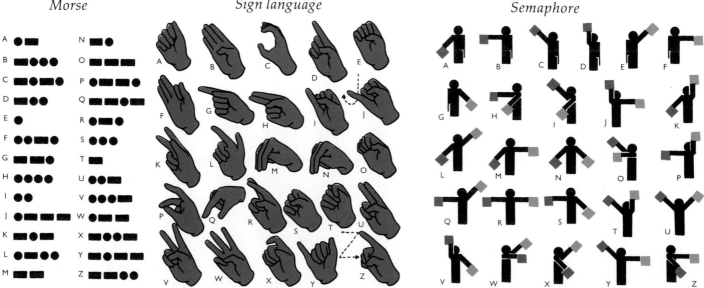

Morse   *Sign language*   *Semaphore*

A one-handed egg cup

- Imagine that you have to make an egg cup for someone who has only one hand. Think about the problems you would have eating a boiled egg with one hand.
- Design an egg cup that would make it easier for you to eat the egg.
- Explain how your design solves some of the problems.
- If you can, make a model of your egg cup from simple materials.
- Test your design. How could it be improved?

Technology to the rescue

Science and technology have done a lot to help handicapped people.

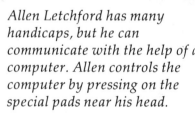

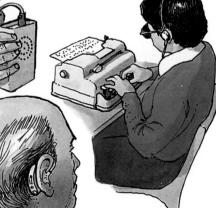

Allen Letchford has many handicaps, but he can communicate with the help of a computer. Allen controls the computer by pressing on the special pads near his head.

- Make a list of the aids shown here.
- Explain who each aid would help and how it would help them.

EXTRAS

1 Design devices for someone who cannot grip things (but can push and pull) to:
(a) turn a tap on and off,
(b) open a can of Coke,
(c) turn a key in a lock.

2 Put your senses in order of their importance to you. Explain why you have put them in that order.

3 Imagine that you have to use Morse or semaphore to send lots of long messages. Make a list of the other signs or symbols you might need. For example, you might need something to tell the receiver that you have made a mistake.

10 SUBSTANCES

10·1 Making new substances

There are many different substances in the world. You have already used several hundred in your science course.

All these substances are made up from a small number of simple chemicals called *elements*. These are the elements that make up your body and the Earth:

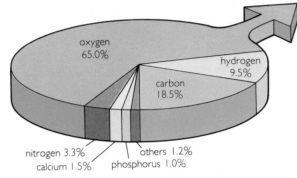

oxygen 65.0%
hydrogen 9.5%
carbon 18.5%
nitrogen 3.3%
calcium 1.5%
phosphorus 1.0%
others 1.2%

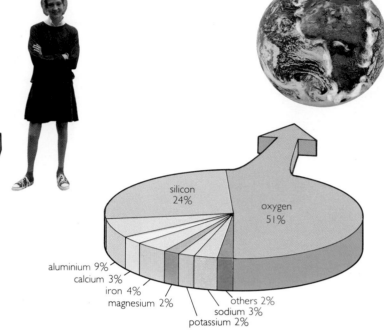

silicon 24%
oxygen 51%
aluminium 9%
calcium 3%
iron 4%
magnesium 2%
potassium 2%
sodium 3%
others 2%

Finding out about substances

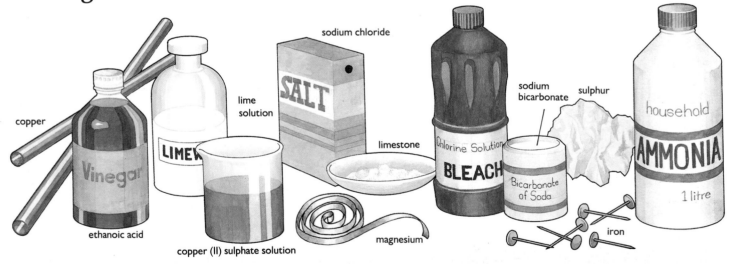

copper

Vinegar
ethanoic acid

LIMEW
lime solution

copper (II) sulphate solution

SALT
sodium chloride

limestone

magnesium

Chlorine Solution
BLEACH

Bicarbonate of Soda
sodium bicarbonate

sulphur

iron

household
AMMONIA
1 litre

Observing

- Look carefully at each of these substances. With your friends you have to divide them into three or four groups. You can touch them, smell them carefully and bend those that will.

Do *not* taste them.

- Write down a title for each group.
- Underneath the title, put the substances in the group.

Changing substances

- With your friends, find out what happens when you mix some of the substances. You must follow these rules:

1. Safety glasses must be worn.

2. Never use more than two substances.

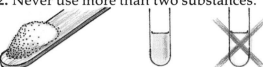

3. Only use a very small quantity of each substance.

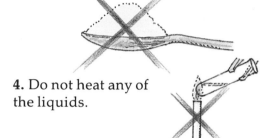

4. Do not heat any of the liquids.

5. Do not taste any of the substances.

6. Smell any gases carefully. If the smell is bad, stop smelling it. Do not make any more of the gas: it could be poisonous.

- Before you start, organise a system for recording your results. You could use a chart or a table.
- If you make a new substance, try to keep a little to show the rest of your class later.
- Are there any patterns in the way that substances mix? Look for these patterns:

1 Which substances often react with others? (*React* means that the substances change.)

2 Which substances do not react much?

3 Is there any link between the way something reacts and the group you put it in earlier?

- Sort each pair of substances that you mixed into three or four groups. You do not have to use the same groups you used before. One group will probably be 'Substances that do nothing'.
- Look at your results. Try to predict what will happen if you do some tests with these two chemicals:
  - sodium carbonate (washing soda). This is a white powder rather like sodium bicarbonate.
  - iron filings (iron wire made into a powder).

You may be able to investigate these substances.

- How do you know if you have made a new substance? Write down a list of things that may happen when something new is made.

EXTRAS

1 Which of these activities do you think make new substances? Explain your answer in each case:
(**a**) striking a match
(**b**) burning a gas flame
(**c**) heating a frying pan
(**d**) frying an egg
(**e**) frying bacon
(**f**) eating a fry-up.

2 Write down ten substances found in your kitchen. Put them into the groups you used on the previous page. Say why you chose the groups you did.

3 Here are some elements that are well-known, but have not been mentioned on this page:

uranium   mercury
hydrogen   iodine
nitrogen   gold

(**a**) Why are they well-known?
(**b**) What are they used for or in?
(**c**) Which ones are rare? Which are common?

10·2 Acids

One important group of substances is called acids. The objects in the display all contain acid. There are many different types, but they behave in the same way.

 ● Find out what happens when you add water or a little weak acid to:
   – washing soda powder (sodium carbonate)
   – beetroot or blackberry juice
   – clean magnesium ribbon
(Do not use battery acid. It is strong and could hurt you.)

● Put the acids you tested in order, with the strongest acid at the top. Include water in the list as well.
● From your investigation, design a way of testing how acid a liquid is.
● Try your test out on liquid from a pickled onion jar, beer or wine, milk.
● Add these liquids to your acidity table.

An acid test ⚠

Here is one way of finding out how acid a liquid is.
● Put a flat spatula of limestone powder in a Petri dish or on a watch glass.
● Add the liquid you want to test, drop by drop.
● Measure how many drops it takes for all the powder to react. The more drops you need, the weaker the acid.

● Before using this test on some acids, think carefully. What will you need to keep the same in each test? How will you do this?

● When you have answered these two questions, measure the acidity of some of your acids. Do you get the same results as before?

Acid fizz

The fizz in fizzy drinks comes from carbon dioxide, which is an acid gas. This usually makes the drink acid (and leads to tooth decay).

- Plan an investigation to find out which drinks are most acidic.
- Check your plan with your teacher and then carry it out.

Man Dissolves Body in Acid

JOHN HAIGH, a 39-year-old company director of South Kensington, London, was today accused of the murder of Mrs Olive Durand-Deacon. She has been missing for two weeks. Her body has not been discovered, and is not likely to be. After killing his victim, Haigh dissolved the body in sulphuric acid.

Haigh admitted the truth to a detective who was sitting with him whilst the two senior investigators were out of the interview room.

Haigh said 'If I told you the truth, you wouldn't believe me.' Detective Inspector Webb cautioned Haigh: 'Anything you say will be taken down . . .'

Haigh interrupted. 'I know all that . . . I'll tell you all about it.

Mrs Durand-Deacon no longer exists. She disappeared completely; no trace of her will ever be found.'

What's happened to her?' Webb enquired.

'I've destroyed her with acid,' came the reply. 'Every trace is gone. How can you accuse me of murder when there is no body?'

But Haigh was found guilty. He was hanged on 6 August 1949 in Wandsworth prison.

EXTRAS

1 Find out which fruits are acid. You could try testing a little juice from a fruit with a pinch of washing soda powder or indigestion tablet powder.

2 Indigestion is a pain in your stomach caused by acid. Find out where the acid comes from, and what usually makes indigestion start.

3 Acids taste sour (but do not try it!). They are used to give some sweets a sharp flavour. If you can, buy some sharp-tasting sweets like acid drops. Dissolve one in a little hot water. Find out if it is acid.

Sometimes acids are very useful to us. Sometimes they do us a lot of harm.
● Acids have had something to do with all the things shown.
  Can you work out how?

1 Which things are useful?

Measuring acidity

There is a special detector of acidity called Universal
Indicator. The colour of the indicator depends on
the strength of the acid it is in. The different
strengths are given a value called a pH number.

Universal Indicator is available as a liquid or as
strips of paper.

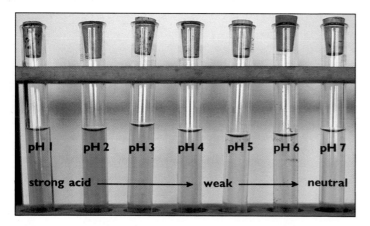

● Use some Universal Indicator paper to
  measure the pH number of some of the acids
  you tested before. Did you get the acidity
  order right?
● Measure the pH number of tap water. Take
  care to use a clean test tube.

Acid rain

Most of Scandinavia is covered with natural pine forests and lakes. The forests are very sensitive to acid in the air. Small amounts can kill the trees. When the acid runs into the lakes it makes them acid, and kills fish and other animals.

Over the last ten years, scientists have noticed more and more damage to trees and water in Scandinavia. Many of them think that it is being caused by acid in the air, mostly from power station

fumes. Because the winds tend to blow from Britain to Scandinavia, some people blame British power stations and factories for the damage.

2 Who is responsible for acid rain? Is it easy to say?

3 Who should do something about it?

4 What should they do?

5 Why don't they do this?

Organism		None	Little	Some	Lots
		How much pollution it can live in			
Mayfly larva		✔			
Stonefly larva		✔			
Caddis fly larva		✔	✔		
Waterlouse		✔	✔	✔	
Sludgeworm		✔	✔	✔	✔
Blanketweed				✔	✔

Is your rain acid?

● Use Universal Indicator to test some rainwater, and some stream and river water near you. It is easier to use Universal Indicator liquid than paper, but you must use very clean test tubes.

● Compare the colour of each of the samples with the colour you get from distilled (pure) water.

The organisms that live in the streams are also a guide to how polluted the water is.

◀ Here are some examples:

EXTRAS

1 Acids cause corrosion and rot. Make a list of things in and outside your house that have corroded.

(**a**) Which things corrode easily?

(**b**) What sort of conditions seem to cause most corrosion?

(**c**) What can be done to stop corrosion?

2 Do a design for a cheap and safe container to carry battery acid in. Label it to show what it is made from.

10·4 Alkalis

Alkalis are a group of substances that are opposite to acids. They cancel acids out. Like acids, they can be both useful and very dangerous.

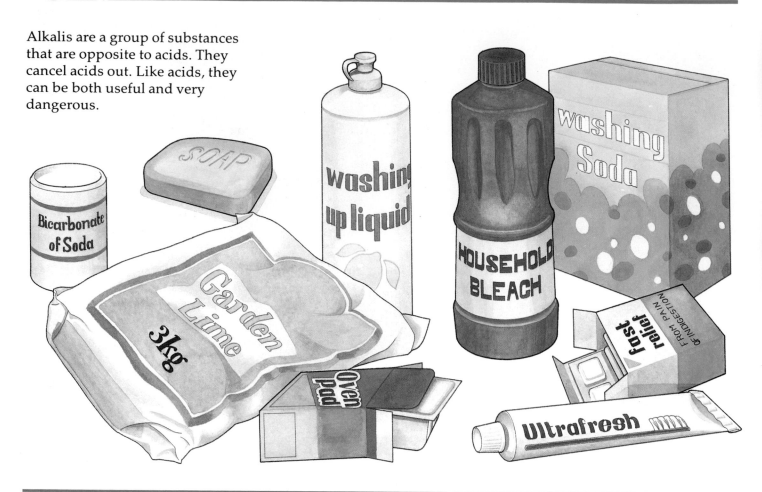

Detecting alkalis ⚠️ 🥽

- Use Universal Indicator paper to test some of the alkalis shown.
- Write down each substance and its pH number. You will have to dampen the indicator paper before testing the solids (it will only work when it is wet).
- Use your results to put the alkalis in order with the most alkaline first.

- Test some of your alkalis with the same substances that you tested acids with:
  - washing soda powder (sodium carbonate)
  - beetroot or blackberry juice
  - clean magnesium ribbon

1 Do they do the same things as acids?

Adding acid to alkali

Universal Indicator liquid is very useful for showing how acid or alkaline something is. The colour changes are like this:

You can use these colours to work out what happens when you add an alkali to an acid.

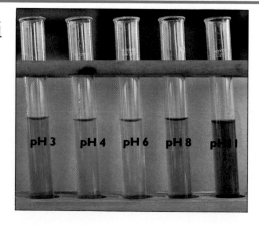

pH 3 pH 4 pH 6 pH 8 pH 1

When you use the indicator liquid, take great care not to contaminate it. Any acid or alkali, even one drop, that gets into the liquid will ruin the whole bottle.

- Half-fill a test tube with an acid solution (clear vinegar or weak hydrochloric acid).
- Add to it a few drops of Universal Indicator solution and stir well.
- Make a solution of sodium bicarbonate in a second test tube.
- Add to it a few drops of Universal Indicator solution and stir well.

- Pour the bicarbonate slowly and carefully into the acid.
- Watch carefully until nothing more happens.
- Write up and explain everything you see.
- If you have time, find out what happens if you do the same thing, but pour acid into the bicarbonate.

Neutralising

If you add just the right amount of alkali to an acid, you can make the liquid neutral. Neutral means that the substances are neither acid nor alkali. Neutral substances have a pH number of 7.

Investigating

Which powder is best?
- Plan an investigation to find out which stomach powder or tablet is best at neutralising acids. Get your plan checked and carry it out.
- **2** Do you think stomach powders should be stronger? Explain your answer.

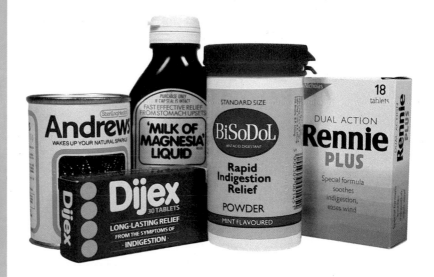

EXTRAS
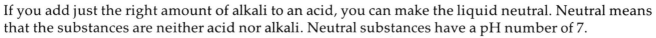

Communicating

1 Alkalis can be just as dangerous as acids. Design a warning poster that gets this message over.

2 The Central Electricity Generating Board is going to clean all the gases produced by power stations in the 1990s.
(a) What is the CEGB trying to get rid of? (Hint: see 10.3)
(b) What should the CEGB use to clean the gases?
(c) How should the CEGB do it? Do a simple design.

3 Officials in Norway and Sweden have been trying to stop the damage from acid rain.
(a) What would you do?
(b) How would you do it?
(c) Who should pay for it?

10·5 Limestone

Limestone is a very common rock. So is chalk, which is a soft type of limestone.

Most limestone was first formed under water. Small animals in the water sank to the seabed when they died. The remains were gradually squashed together to make rock. This process usually takes millions of years.

Since then, the continents have moved. When limestone started forming, Britain was a tropical country quite near the equator. Now it is nearer the North Pole than the equator.

Much of our countryside is limestone that has been raised above sea level. Some of it has been changed by pressure and heat in the earth. Much has been worn away by traces of acid in our rain.

You can find the remains of sea animals in some types of limestone.

Limelight ⚠️ 👓

● Heat a limestone chip in a hot Bunsen flame.
● Look carefully at the chip. You may see it glow when it gets hot. Before electricity, lime was used for lighting, particularly in theatres. This is where the phrase 'in the limelight' comes from.

● After ten minutes, turn the Bunsen off. Let the hot chip cool down.
● Try to find as many differences as you can between the heated chip and a fresh limestone chip.

1 Do they look different?
2 Which scratches most easily?
3 What happens to one drop of water on each chip?
4 Does the chip make the water drop acid or alkaline?
5 What happens to a drop of dilute acid on the chip?

Heating limestone strongly changes it into quicklime. Quicklime is an alkali that is used by farmers to make soil less acid. It has also been put into Swedish lakes to neutralise acid rain.

An acid spill

'All I saw was a puff of smoke coming from his front wheel . . . Then he swerved across the road and hit the tree.'

'What speed was he travelling at, sir?' asked the policewoman.

'About 50, I think.'

The witness did not know much more. Acid was leaking from a huge hole in the tanker where it had hit the tree. The smell was awful, and the road had started to bubble. The Chief Fire Officer had to decide whether to neutralise the acid or to hose it away into the drains.

'Have we got much lime with us?' he asked another officer.

'Enough to neutralise most of what's spilt so far, sir. Can't do any harm to put it down – we can hose it later.'

'You're right,' said the Chief. 'Carry on.'

● Investigate the best substance to use to neutralise an acid spill. You can use a very little dilute mineral acid as a model spill and test different chemicals on it. Find out:
  – what is safe to carry and use
  – what is fairly cheap
  – whether it is best to use lumps, powder or liquid
  – what could leave the spill neutral

Cost of some chemicals (per kilogram) you may test:
limestone chips 80p
ammonia £4.50
water (very cheap)
quicklime powder £2.20
sodium carbonate £3.60
sodium chloride £2.00

● Write a short report for the Chief Fire Officer.

6 What damage might be caused if you used the cheapest method?

Quarrying limestone

Limestone comes from quarries. The quarries are usually in attractive countryside. They have to be carefully managed to preserve the environment.

7 Why do you think the use of limestone has increased since 1910?

8 How much do you think we will be using in the year 2000?

9 What will happen in the limestone areas of Britain if your forecast in question 8 is right?

10 How would you 'carefully manage' a quarry to preserve the environment?

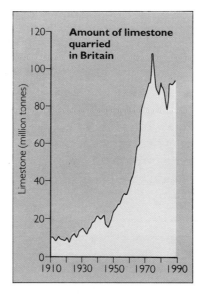

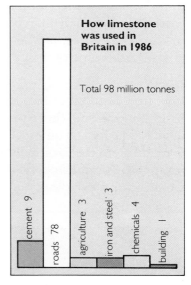

EXTRAS

1 Chalk, marble, calcite, seashells and eggshell are all made from the same chemical as limestone. Plan an investigation to show how you could check this.

2 Some buildings, like the Houses of Parliament, are built from limestone. What are the advantages and disadvantages of using limestone for building? The photo may give you one clue.

dirty   clean

10·6 Iron and steel

Working with iron

Iron is an element that is not found on its own in the Earth. It is always joined to other elements, usually oxygen. This mixture is called *iron ore*.

Separating iron from iron ore is quite hard. Humans have been able to do it for about 3000 years. At first, they used wood in charcoal furnaces. These made small amounts of soft iron.

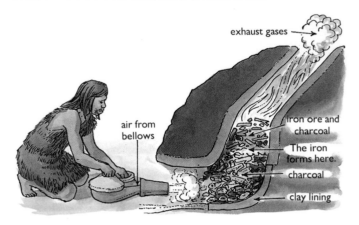

Cast iron

In the 1700s people found that coke, a type of coal, worked better than charcoal. They used it to make cast iron. Cast iron can be poured into moulds, and it is a harder type of iron than soft iron.

Steel

Cast iron cannot be shaped by machines, and it is brittle. In Europe, these problems were solved just over 100 years ago when steel was first made. Steel is made from cast iron when some impurities are removed. Special steels can be made by adding small amounts of other elements.

At the Wuhan steelworks in China.

Some types of iron and steel

Type	Element added	Used for
Wrought iron	None	Gates and decorations
Cast iron	None	Car engine blocks
Mild steel	¼% carbon	Cans and buckets
High carbon steel	1–4% carbon	Razor blades, saws
Nickel steel	Nickel	Carrying acids, machinery
Stainless steel	Nickel and chrome	Cutlery, long-life exhausts
Titanium steel	Titanium	Concorde's fuselage
Tungsten steel	Tungsten	High-speed drills

● Choose the type of iron or steel you would use for the jobs listed. Explain your choices.

1. a garden spade
2. a Bunsen burner base
3. a towing cable
4. a sharp kitchen knife
5. a space rocket
6. a car body

Observing

Burning iron ⚠ 🥽
● Set up the equipment (Bunsen, heatproof mat, spatula).
● Put the Bunsen on a blue flame. Hold the spatula with the iron powder well above the flame.
● Tap the iron powder off the spatula into the flame.
● Repeat this, but with iron filings instead of powder.
● Hold some steel wool in tongs in the flame.
● Hold an iron nail in tongs in the flame. (**Care** – hot!)
● Write down all you see.
● Try to explain any differences between the types of iron you have used.

Rust

Every year, one-fifth of the iron in the world is destroyed by rust. Rust does millions of pounds of damage in Britain alone. Many people and companies spend a lot of money trying to stop it.

Every new car that is made is rust-proofed with paint and special sealers. But cars still rust in the end. Look at these survey results:

Percentage of all cars with serious rust in the parts listed

Age of car (years)	1	2	3	4	5	6	7	8
Suspension/springs	0	0	0	0	1	1	1	3
Floor	0	0	0	1	1	3	6	9
Doors	0	1	2	3	6	8	10	15
Door sills	0	1	3	4	8	14	19	27
Frong wings	0	1	3	5	12	17	24	32
Rear wings	0	0	1	2	4	4	6	11
Box sections	0	0	0	0	2	2	4	5
Jacking point	0	0	0	0	1	2	4	7
Overall	0	3	7	14	26	34	44	58

This means that 58%, well over half, of all eight-year-old cars have serious rust.

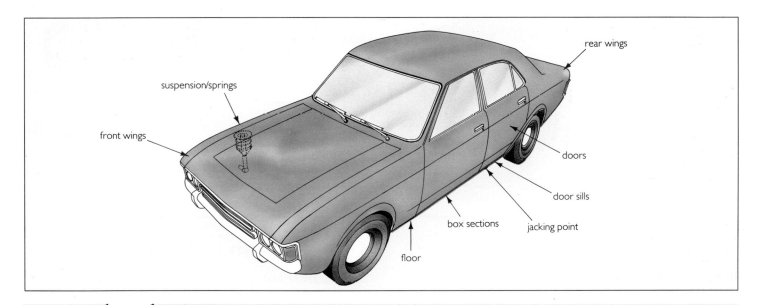

Communicating

1 What percentage of cars have rust in the rear wings after 7 years?

2 Where does most rusting happen?

3 If you were buying a three-year-old car, where would you look for rust?

4 Do a bar chart to show where eight-year-old cars have rust.

5 A jacking point on a car is where you put a jack to raise the car. What could happen if you wanted to jack up a car that is six years old?

6 Make a list of all the things you can do to stop a car from rusting.

EXTRAS

1 Carry out a survey of cars in your area. You could make a short questionnaire for parents and friends who have cars. Find out if your results are the same as the survey on this page.

2 Choose a metal (not iron or steel) and find out all you can about it. How is it obtained from the earth? What is it used for?

3 Choose a car part from the table. Draw a graph to show what percentage of cars have serious rust in that part as they get older.

4 Which parts of a bike rust fastest? What can you do to stop it?

10·7 Copper

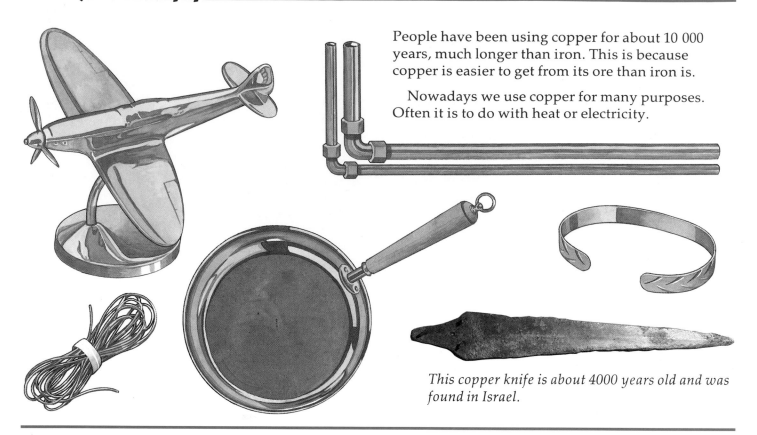

People have been using copper for about 10 000 years, much longer than iron. This is because copper is easier to get from its ore than iron is.

Nowadays we use copper for many purposes. Often it is to do with heat or electricity.

This copper knife is about 4000 years old and was found in Israel.

Making copper ⚠ 🥽

In each of these experiments you can make copper metal from a substance that contains copper.

- Observe each one carefully. How do you know you have made copper each time?
- Put a clean piece of magnesium ribbon into a test tube containing copper (II) sulphate solution.
- Connect two carbon rods to a power pack (at 6V or less) or battery. Dip them into copper (II) sulphate solution. Don't let them touch! ▶

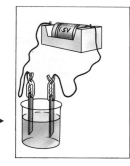

- Mix a spatula of copper (II) oxide with a spatula of charcoal in a crucible. Heat strongly for five minutes. ▶
- Put a spatula of iron filings into a test tube of copper (II) sulphate solution.

Your teacher may show you a more dangerous way of getting copper from copper (II) oxide using iron.

Copper from copper ore

This chart shows how pure copper is made.

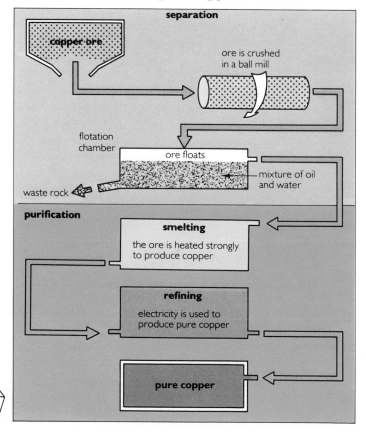

Heating copper ⚠️ 🥽

- Clean four strips of copper with emery paper or steel wool.
- Paint clear nail varnish on one and let it dry.
- Put the second strip next to the first one.
- Heat the third strip in a blue Bunsen flame for 1 minute. Leave it to cool.
- Fold the fourth strip in half.
- Seal the edges by turning them over so that no air or flame can reach the copper inside the strip.
- Heat the fourth strip like the third one.
- When it is cool, open it so that the copper inside is facing up.
- Very carefully compare the four strips.
- Write down how each strip was treated, and what it looks like:

> 3.3.00 <u>Heating copper strips</u>
>
> <u>Strip 1</u>
> This was coated in nail varnish so no air could get to it. It looks shiny and clean.
>
> <u>Strip 2</u>
> This ...

Copper facts

Here are some facts about copper:

- copper is not a very reactive metal

- copper oxide is black

- there is oxygen in the air

- heating makes things react faster.

Use these facts and your experiment to answer the questions:

1. What does cold air do to copper?
2. What should you do to be more certain of your answer to question 1?
3. What makes copper change when it gets hot?
4. Why is the inside of piece number four different from the outside?
5. What investigation could you do to check your answer to question 4?
6. Is copper more or less reactive than iron? How could you find out?

EXTRAS

1. Plumbers used to make water pipes from lead because lead is easy to bend and join. Now they use plastic pipes and copper pipes.
(a) Why is lead not used any more?
(b) Why is copper used?
(c) Why is plastic used sometimes?

2. Make a list of all the places in your house that copper is used. There is copper in the alloys bronze and brass, as well as in copper-nickel coins.

10·8 Sulphur

Sulphur is an element that is mined by being melted underground and then pumped up. Here you can see a sulphur works in Canada.

Iron and sulphur

- Find out all the differences you can between iron and sulphur. You can use an iron nail or iron filings. Try strength, scratch, a magnet, electricity, floating and measuring.
- Mix some iron filings with a little sulphur powder. Find a good way to separate them.

Your teacher may show you what happens when a mixture of sulphur and iron is heated. You cannot do it yourself safely because heated sulphur makes poisonous fumes of sulphur dioxide.

Heated iron and sulphur cannot be separated. The iron and sulphur react to make a new substance called iron sulphide. Iron sulphide is a *compound*; it is made from more than one element.

Copper and sulphur

Here is Katie's report about heating a coil of copper wire with some sulphur.

Heating copper and sulphur

We heated the copper wire in the middle of the tube. After a while it got red hot. Then we heated the sulphur. At first there was an awful smell, then the sulphur bubbled. Next the copper went bright red and the tube filled with brown smoke.

When it cooled down, we emptied the tube. A black coil dropped out. When we picked up the coil it broke in half. It was covered in black crystals. There was no sulphur left at all.

- Write a description of the copper and sulphur before Katie heated them.
- Write a description of the substance she has made.

1 What do you think the substance Katie made is called?

- Katie has not done a drawing for her experiment. Use her report to draw what you think she did.

2 Katie has said nothing about safety. What safety precautions would you have taken?

Sulphur dioxide

When sulphur burns it makes a gas called sulphur dioxide. This gas is choking and poisonous, but it can be useful. It is used to make sulphuric acid, to make paper, for bleaching and to kill microbes.

One way of making sulphur dioxide is to burn sulphur in air. This is dangerous. You can make the gas safely by putting a Campden tablet in water. The sulphur dioxide it gives off dissolves in the water and is safe.

- Test some dissolved sulphur dioxide. Find out
  - if it is acid or alkali.
  - which materials it can bleach the colour from.
  - if it works on some colours better than others.
  - if it helps to keep the bleaching solution warm.

Sulphur particles are so tiny that you cannot see what happens to them when a lump of sulphur burns. You would need to magnify it about 10 million times! When sulphur particles are heated, they link up with oxygen from the air.

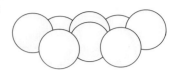

Sulphur is made of only one kind of particle, so it is an *element*. The particles, called atoms, are joined together in rings.

Oxygen is also an element. It is made of oxygen atoms joined in pairs.

When sulphur and oxygen are heated, the atoms separate and make a new *compound*, sulphur dioxide. Sulphur dioxide has two oxygen atoms joined to each sulphur atom.

Investigating

Keeping food fresh

Sulphur dioxide is a preservative. It is used to stop food from going off.

- Carry out an investigation to find out how quickly the inside of an apple goes brown once it is cut.
- Then find out the smallest amount of sulphur dioxide solution that is needed to stop this.

3 What other ways can you find to stop an apple from going brown?

4 Which do you think is best? Why?

EXTRAS

1 Do a design for a device that will separate a mixture of iron and sulphur. Your device should be able to cope with a stream of mixture, and get both elements back.

2 Sulphur is a *non-metal*. Copper and iron are both metals. Make a list of non-metals and a list of metals. Then make a list of words that describe non-metals, and a list of words that describe metals.

3 Sulphur dioxide is often added to food. Any food with E220 on the label contains it. Find as many foods as you can which have sulphur dioxide added as a preservative.

The proper name for common salt is sodium chloride. It is a compound of two elements: sodium and chlorine. Salt is all around us:
– you put it on your chips
– there's a lot of it in the sea
– it's sprayed on to our roads to stop them freezing
– it's used to make other chemicals like chlorine and caustic soda.

Salt is found underground in Britain. To bring it to the surface, we usually dissolve it in water to make brine and pump the liquid up. We then evaporate the water to get the salt. Some salt is mined by using diggers underground in enormous tunnels.

Rock salt contains salt mixed up with grit and rock.

Purifying rock salt
● Plan a method to make a lump of rock salt into pure table salt. Some of these processes may help you (but you must change the order!).
 – dissolve
 – evaporate slowly   – crush
 – stir   – filter

● Make a flow chart from your plan that shows what you will do. Get your plan approved.
● Use your plan to investigate how much table salt you can get from 50g of rock salt.
● Write up your method and your results.
● Suggest anything you could do to get more salt from your rock salt.

Salt facts

Two hundred million years ago much of the Midlands was covered by sea. The climate was hot, and the sea gradually dried. It left behind layers of salt crystals. Since then, the salt layers have been covered by clay and sand. But in Cheshire and Shropshire, the salt is near the surface and can be mined.

The Romans knew this, and made salt from brine. Brine forms underground when salt dissolves in water. The Romans got salt back by heating the brine. Salt was used to preserve food; it was a very important chemical.

In the 18th and 19th centuries, salt was first used to make other chemicals. Demand for salt grew. This is when people started to pump water underground to dissolve the salt and pump out the brine. Unfortunately, this caused some problems: look at the photograph.

Salt is now mined as rock salt in a mine 150 metres deep in Winsford, Cheshire. It is also pumped out as brine, but with care to stop subsidence.

Houses in Northwich collapsed because so much salt had been removed from under the ground.

1 What would you have done to stop the houses in Northwich from collapsing?

2 Why is brine easier to get from the ground than rock salt?

3 The word *salary* comes from Roman salt mining times. What is the connection between salt and salary?

● Make a flow chart that shows how the Romans may have made salt.

Corrosion

Rock salt is not purified. It is used for gritting roads. One problem of using salt for this job is that it helps things to rust.

Investigating

● Plan investigations to find out which of these statements are right. Get your plans approved, then carry them out. You could do your tests on clean iron nails. Be patient: they may take several days.
  – Salt needs water to corrode steel.
  – Only a trace of salt is needed to speed up corrosion.
  – Rock salt is less corrosive than pure salt.
  – Air is needed for something to rust.
  – Hot salt water corrodes faster than cold.
  – Other salts (like Epsom salts, magnesium sulphate) corrode things as well.

EXTRAS

1 Salt is very important in hot countries. Think of reasons why. Where do countries that have no underground salt get their salt from?

2 Investigate why salt is put on icy roads. (Use two lumps of ice from the fridge as a model.)

3 What shape are salt crystals? Draw a large picture of two or three different crystals.

10·10 Chlorine

Chlorine is a very important element. It is made by passing electricity through sodium chloride solution.

● Set up this equipment:

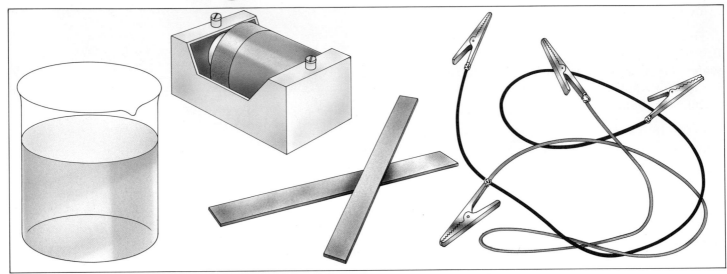

● Dip the rods in the water and watch. Do not let them touch.
● Ask a friend to stir a spatula of sodium chloride into the water. Keep watching.

● Find out:
  – if the water near each rod is acid or alkali;
  – if the gases smell (smell carefully!);
  – if the gases are acid or alkaline. (Hold damp indicator paper over the water.)

● Try to collect the gas which comes faster from the rods. Here is one way to do it: ▶
● When you have a tube full of gas, take the tube out and put a stopper over the end. Hold a lit spill above the end of the tube, then take the stopper away.

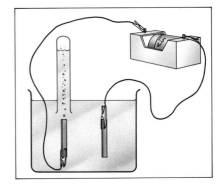

Use your results and the information below to decide what the gases are:

oxygen – neutral/no smell/relights a glowing spill/makes a lit spill burn brightly

hydrogen – neutral/no smell/ 'pops' when lit in air

nitrogen – neutral/no smell/ puts flames out

chlorine – bleaches/its smell is typical of swimming baths/slight green colour

carbon dioxide – just acid/no smell/ puts flames out/makes limewater go milky

sulphur dioxide – acid/choking smell/ puts flames out

ammonia – alkali/wet nappy smell/ puts flames out

● Investigate if water which has chlorine dissolved in it can bleach coloured material or paper.
● Find out which materials and colours it works best with.

Making tonnes of chlorine

In factories, chlorine is made from salt in the same way that you made it. In the factory, chlorine gas must be kept away from one of the other products, sodium hydroxide. If they meet, they combine to make bleach.

So the places where the two chemicals are made have to be separate. One way of doing this is to use an asbestos sheet or *diaphragm*. This screen lets the electricity flow through, but does not let the chemicals mix.

In a factory, each cell contains several pairs of electrodes. The whole factory may have hundreds of cells in total.

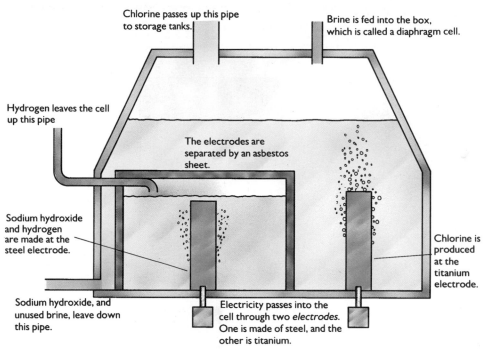

Chlorine passes up this pipe to storage tanks.

Brine is fed into the box, which is called a diaphragm cell.

Hydrogen leaves the cell up this pipe

The electrodes are separated by an asbestos sheet.

Sodium hydroxide and hydrogen are made at the steel electrode.

Chlorine is produced at the titanium electrode.

Sodium hydroxide, and unused brine, leave down this pipe.

Electricity passes into the cell through two *electrodes*. One is made of steel, and the other is titanium.

● Make a list of the parts of a diaphragm cell.
● Next to each part, write down what you used to do the same job in your experiment. You may not be able to do this for all the parts.

Using chlorine

Chlorine is used in many important jobs.

You can find 'chlor-' in many chemical names.

Chlorine is a dangerous gas. It has to be stored and used carefully. If you breathe chlorine, it attacks the lining of your lungs and stops you from breathing. Chlorine was used to make mustard gas that was used in World War 1. This gas caused horrific injuries to people affected by it.

EXTRAS

1 What has household bleach got to do with chlorine?

2 If you were a British scientist in 1914, would you have helped to develop mustard gas?

Why do you think it was made? Why did the countries fighting in World War 2 agree not to use poison gases?

3 You used test tubes and carbon rods to collect the gases from passing electricity through brine. Design a better way to collect the gases.

rocks that contain water

major reservoirs

pipelines from reservoirs to cities

0   100km

N

Glasgow

Belfast

Newcastle-upon-Tyne

Middlesbrough

Leeds

Liverpool

Nottingham

Birmingham

Cardiff

London

Our drinking water comes from many different places. It is never completely pure; there are always other chemicals dissolved in it. The investigations on this page are about the chemicals that you find in water.

Pure water

Pure water is made from tap water by distillation.
- Find out what elements pure water is made from by passing electricity through it. Use the same equipment you used for passing electricity through brine.
- First try pure water on its own. It should not conduct electricity if it is pure. Add a few drops of dilute sulphuric acid to make it a conductor.
- Collect the gases that come from each of the carbon rods.
- Use the information about gases on 10.10 to decide what they are.

1 What elements is water made from?

Planning

Chemicals in water
- Plan an investigation to measure the amount of dissolved chemicals in some of these samples of water:
  - your tap water
  - distilled water
  - 'hard' water
  - sea water
  - mineral water
- Check your plan with your teacher, then carry it out.
- When you have done it, test the chemicals dissolved in the samples. Add a drop of dilute hydrochloric acid to each one in turn. If it fizzes, the sample probably contains a carbonate.

Hard and soft water

Drinking water is either hard or soft. Both look the same, but they are quite different when you add a little soap to them.

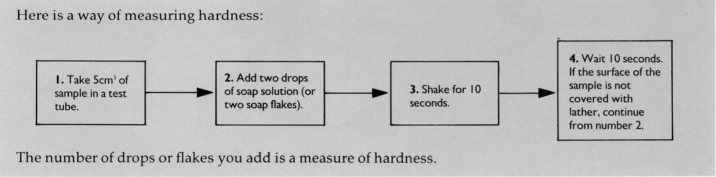

Here is a way of measuring hardness:

1. Take 5cm³ of sample in a test tube. → **2.** Add two drops of soap solution (or two soap flakes). → **3.** Shake for 10 seconds. → **4.** Wait 10 seconds. If the surface of the sample is not covered with lather, continue from number 2.

The number of drops or flakes you add is a measure of hardness.

- Test some samples of water to find out which are hard and which are soft. [W]

Getting rid of hardness

Hard water is a nuisance. It is awkward to use for washing, and it blocks pipes.

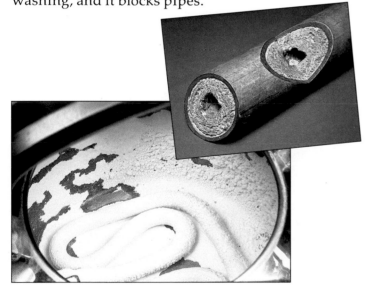

There are four ways of getting rid of hardness:
1. Boiling the water (this only works with some types of water). ⚠
2. Using a water softener. This replaces the elements that cause hardness.

3. Adding washing soda to the water.
4. Adding a water softening powder to the water.

- Plan an investigation to find out which of these methods is best for softening water. Get your plan approved, then carry it out.
- Write a report on 'How to soften water'.

EXTRAS

1 Look at this diagram of a *fuel cell*. Write a short article for a science magazine for 13-year-olds about fuel cells. Explain what fuel cells are, what they could be used for and how they work.

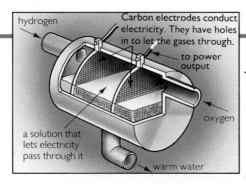

hydrogen
Carbon electrodes conduct electricity. They have holes in to let the gases through.
to power output
oxygen
a solution that lets electricity pass through it
warm water

◄ *In a fuel cell, hydrogen and oxygen join together. When this happens, they make heat and electricity.*

2 Carry out an investigation to find out if rain water is hard or soft.

11 FORCES
11:1 Using force

All these people are using forces.

● Write down ten things you do every day that use forces.

● Then with a group of friends write down as many words as you can think of that describe force. The first one might be *push*.

Measuring forces

Meters that measure forces usually have springs in them. The bigger the force, the more the spring is squashed or stretched. The amount of squash or stretch is measured in newtons.

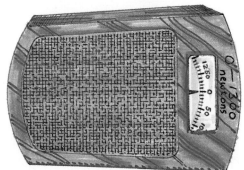

● Find out how much force you need to do some of these jobs. Take care to use the right meter for the right job. You may need some extra equipment for some of the tests.
● Draw up a table for your results.
  – Pull a stool along the floor.
  – Pull a rubber band to twice its length.
  – Squash a sponge to half its thickness.
  – Open a door.
  – Twist a sponge half-way round.
  – Operate a push-button pen.
  – Turn a water tap on (**care!**) ⚠
  – Remove a push-on lid from a tin.
  – Open a bulldog clip or a clothes peg.
  – Lift a 1 kilogram mass from the floor to the bench.

● Add a few jobs of your own to this list.
● Compare your group's results with other people's results.

1 Do you think your results are accurate?
2 What could you do to get better results?

A long stretch

Try this:

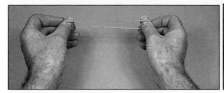 

● Stretch a rubber band a little in your hands.

● Then stretch it a long way.

3 Do you need *more* or *less* force than before to stretch it a long way?

● Plan an experiment to find out how the force changes as you stretch the band. Get your plan checked and carry it out. You should aim to make a graph from your experiment:

Stretch of band (cm) — Pulling force (N)

Big forces

MINERVA, THE CHAMPION STRONG WOMAN.

HOLDER OF THE RICHARD K. FOX CHAMPIONSHIP BELT AND THE POLICE GAZETTE GOLD CUP, FOR HEAVYWEIGHT LIFTING.

In 1957, Paul Anderson used a force of almost 30 000 N to lift a weight off trestles. This is the greatest lift recorded by a man.

Because of their different body structure, women cannot lift as much as men. The biggest lifting force ever used by a woman was just over 15 000 N by Josephine Blatt in 1895.

● Work out how many strong men or women it would take to lift these things:

– a Harrier jump jet off the ground (weight 100 000 N)
– a jumbo jet off the ground (weight 3 800 000 N)
– a Saturn V rocket off its launch pad (weight 35 000 000 N)

EXTRAS

1 Find a job which needs a force of exactly 1 N.

2 Sometimes forces have to be small:

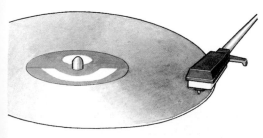

Sometimes too big a force will break something:

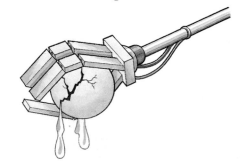

Write down a list of jobs that you think need a force of less than 1 newton.

3 Make a list of five forces used in your kitchen. Make an estimate of the size of each force.

How do springs stretch?

- Make a spring from some fairly thick copper wire. Use 50cm of wire and wrap it round the rod of a laboratory stand.
- Take your spring off the stand and test it. ⚠
- Your job is to find out how the length of the spring depends on the weight that is hung on it.
- Write your results down in a table as you go along. Stop when your spring goes out of shape.

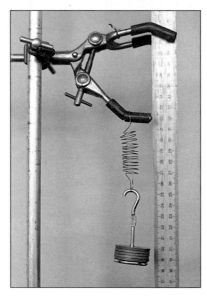

What is the best way of displaying your results? Is it on:
- a pie chart?
- a bar chart?
- a line graph?
- Pick the one you think is best.
- Make a big poster that shows your group's work and displays your results.

- Look at everybody else's poster. Is yours good?

1 How could you improve it?
- Find out if a proper spring stretches like your home-made spring.

Clothes pegs

Some clothes pegs have springs in them. Others work because of the springiness of the stuff that they are made from.

- Plan investigations to answer these questions: ⚠ 😎
  - How strong does a clothes peg need to be to stop washing from blowing away?
  - Which type of clothes peg is strongest?
  - Which type of peg is best for the job? Take care not to break the pegs you test!

Get your plans checked and carry them out.

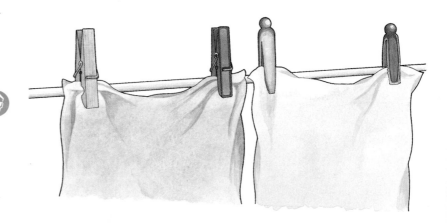

Springs for different jobs

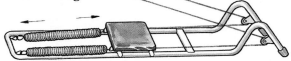

Springs are used in three ways:

– stretching

– squashing   – twisting

- Look at the springs on this page. Think of other things that use springs. Then try these tasks:
- Make a list of springs that are used for stretching (*tension* springs).
- Make a list of springs that are used for squashing (*compression* springs).
- Make a list of springs that are used for twisting (*torsion* springs).
- Put all the springs in order, with the strongest first.
- **2** What happens if a spring is too weak for its job?
- **3** What happens if a spring is too strong for its job?

Investigating

Changing the strength of a spring

You have to find out what it is that decides how 'springy' a spring is. Is it:
– the number of coils?   – the width of the coils?

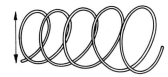

– or the size of the wire?

- Use the same sort of home-made spring that you made before. But plan before you start. Think carefully what you will keep the same, what you will alter and what you will measure. Get your plan approved first.

EXTRAS

1 You are a pram designer and you have to design a child's pram to go over rough ground. How would you design the springs?

2 Design and make a model trampoline from rubber bands. Use card as a frame, and a piece of polythene for the trampoline bed. Which is the most difficult bit to make? How could your model help someone who makes real trampolines?

3 Which things at home have springs in? Make a list.

Sir Isaac Newton

Isaac Newton was a genius. He was born in Lincolnshire in 1642. A poet wrote this about him:

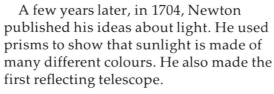

'Nature and Nature's laws lay hid in night: God said, 'Let Newton be!' and all was light.'

These four British stamps show Newton's important discoveries:

Newton's most famous book is called the *Principia*. It is about gravity, the force that pulls things to the ground. The stamp shows an apple because it is said that when Newton saw an apple fall from a tree he got the idea of gravity. The newton, the unit of force which is named after him, is roughly equal to the pull of the Earth on an apple.

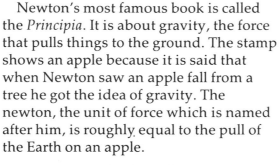

Newton used his law of gravity to explain why planets move in ellipses round the Sun. An ellipse is a squashed circle; the dashed line on the stamp is an ellipse.

A few years later, in 1704, Newton published his ideas about light. He used prisms to show that sunlight is made of many different colours. He also made the first reflecting telescope.

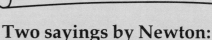

After Newton died in 1727, another book of his about gravity was published. This explains how objects move. The ideas in this book form the basic laws of motion that are taught in schools today. Amongst other things, Newton was able to predict how satellites could orbit the Earth over 200 years before any actually did.

Two sayings by Newton:

'If I have seen further than other men it is because I have stood on the shoulders of giants.'

'I seem to have been only like a boy playing on the seashore, diverting myself now and then by finding a smoother pebble or a prettier shell than ordinary, whilst the great ocean of truth lay all undiscovered before me.'

- Describe carefully each of the postage stamps. Explain how the things you describe are connected with Sir Isaac Newton.
- There are four quotations on this page. Two are by Newton, and two are about Newton. Explain in your own words what you think each one means.

And one about him:

'If he has not been minded, he would go very carelessly, with his shoes down at the heels, stockings untied, head scarcely combed.'

Force and weight

Weight is just a special sort of force caused by the Earth attracting everything on it or near it.

- Use a spring or a rubber band to make a weighing machine that measures the pull of the Earth on objects. You will need to make a scale for it.
- Weigh some objects with your machine.
- Write a report on your machine and your results.

Weight in the solar system

View of the Earth rising, taken by Apollo 8 astronauts on the moon.

The pull of gravity is different in parts of the solar system.

Planet or body	Mass of planet, taking the Earth as 100*	Average distance from the Sun (million km)	Pull of gravity on a 1kg mass on the planet's surface (newtons)
Mercury	6	60	4
Venus	80	105	9
Earth	100	150	10
Mars	10	230	4
Jupiter	31 700	770	26
Saturn	9 500	1 400	11
Earth's Moon	1	150	1.7

*The mass of the Earth is 6000 million million million tonnes!

Communicating

Study the information in the table.

1 Which planet has the biggest mass?

2 Which planet is closest to the Sun?

3 (a) What is the pull of gravity on a 1 kilogram bag of sugar on Earth?
(b) What would it be on Mars?
(c) On which planet would the pull be the greatest?

4 Rachel weighs 40kg. What would be the pull of gravity on her on Venus?

5 On which of the planets/moons would you be able to jump the highest?

6 Bob wrote this: 'The further a planet is from the Sun, the bigger the pull of gravity on it.' Is he right? Explain your answer.

EXTRAS

1 What force do you press on the ground with?

2 Astronaut Neil Armstrong was the first man on the Moon. He weighed 75 kilograms on Earth.

(a) With what force did he push down on the Earth?
(b) With what force do you think he made his footprints on the Moon? Explain your answer.

3 Here is one way of writing Newton's first law of motion: 'Things stay as they are, either moving or still, unless a force affects them.'

Give some practical examples to show what this means.

11·4 Forces at work

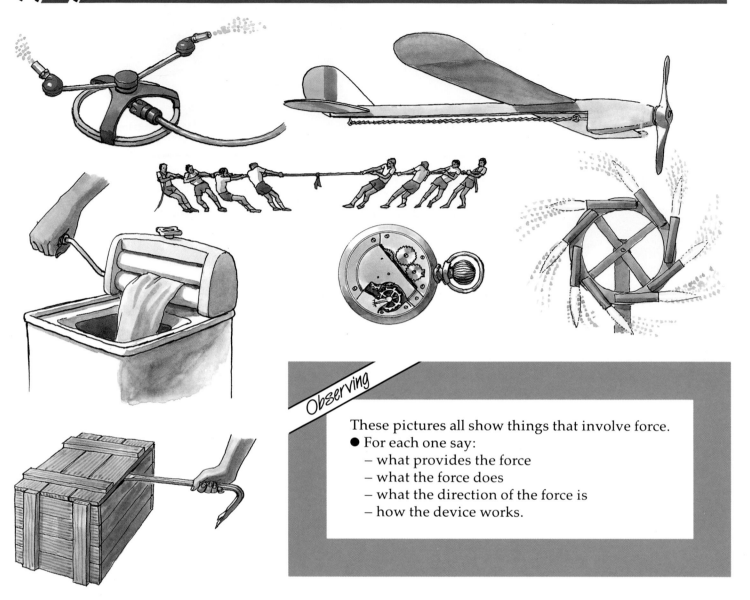

Observing

These pictures all show things that involve force.
● For each one say:
  – what provides the force
  – what the force does
  – what the direction of the force is
  – how the device works.

Levers

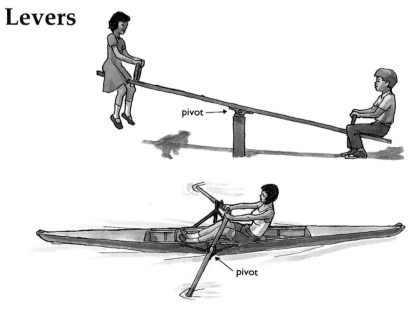

pivot

pivot

● Make a lever from a piece of wood.

● Use some of these objects to answer this question: 'How does the force needed to lift a weight depend on where the pivot is?'
  – a newton meter
  – some 100g masses
  – a 30cm ruler
  – an elastic band
  – some string

● Work with a friend. Produce a report on your investigation.
● Think of a good way to display your results for the rest of your class to see.

Levels in action

These three devices all contain levers.

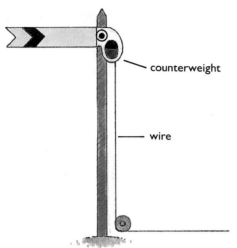

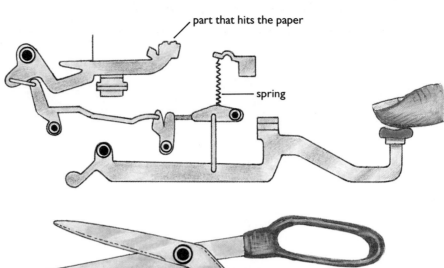

part that hits the paper

spring

- Do a good sketch of each device.
- Mark any pivots with red.
- Draw a blue arrow on each to show where you have to push it to make it work.
- Draw green arrows to show the direction that the parts move.

The railway signal

1 Why has it got a counterweight?

When the signal is 'up' the line is clear, when it is level it means stop. If the signal wiring goes wrong, the signal must 'fail safe'.

2 What does this mean?
3 How would you design the signal so that it 'fails safe'?

The scissors

4 Where is the cutting force greatest? (You could test this with some paper, but take care.)
5 How would you re-design the scissors to cut thicker things? Do a sketch.

The typewriter key

6 How many levers are there in one typewriter key?
7 What is the job of the spring?
8 Make a flowchart to describe what happens when the key is pressed.

EXTRAS

small force on lever

large force to get tyre over rim

1 With most levers you use a small force to make or move a larger force.
(**a**) Draw some other levers you use that are like this.
(**b**) On each drawing, mark on the pivot.
(**c**) Which moves further, the small force you use or the larger force you are moving?

2 The lid of this tin has stuck on. Do a labelled sketch to show how you could get it off. You must use as little force as possible.

11:5 Levers in your body

Bones

There are over 200 bones in your body. The bones meet at joints that let the bones move. So the bones can be levers, with the joint as a pivot. You can see how this works on your arm.

When the biceps muscle gets shorter, it pulls the lower arm bones up. The elbow is the pivot and the lower arm bones are the lever.

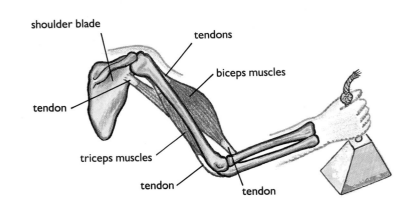

shoulder blade
tendons
biceps muscles
tendon
triceps muscles
tendon
tendon

Tissues

There are three important *tissues* linked to your skeleton. None of them is as hard as bone, but they are all strong.

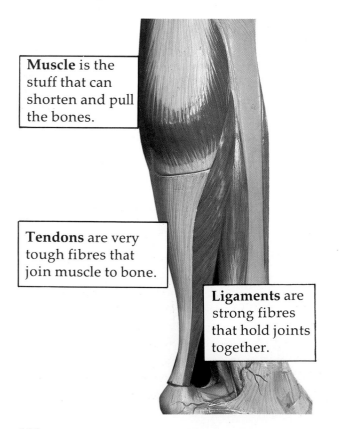

Muscle is the stuff that can shorten and pull the bones.

Tendons are very tough fibres that join muscle to bone.

Ligaments are strong fibres that hold joints together.

A model arm

- Make a model arm from a stand and clamp.
- Investigate what force you have to use in the 'biceps' to lift some different loads. You could try loads between 100g and 1kg.
- The strongest arm in the world has pulled a load of about 350kg. Can you make an estimate from your results of the force in the puller's biceps?

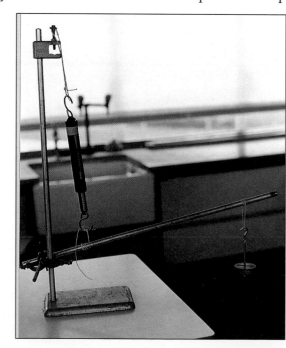

Joints

There are four types of joint in your body:

Sliding joints

The two parts can move a small amount in any direction.

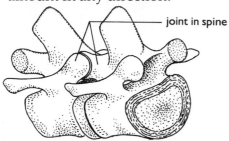

joint in spine

Hinge joints

The two parts can move a long way in one direction.

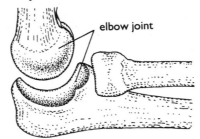

elbow joint

Pivot joints

The two top parts can turn round on each other. The joint between the head and the neck is an example of a pivot joint.

Ball and socket joints

The two parts can turn in any direction.

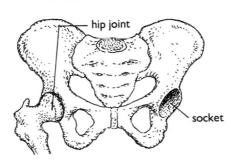

hip joint

socket

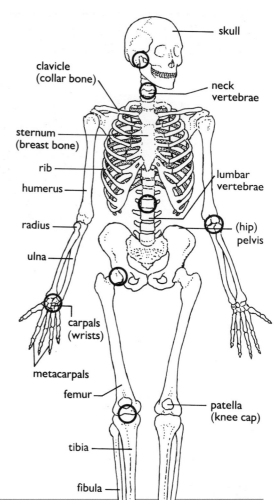

skull

clavicle (collar bone)

neck vertebrae

sternum (breast bone)

rib

humerus

lumbar vertebrae

radius

(hip) pelvis

ulna

carpals (wrists)

metacarpals

femur

patella (knee cap)

tibia

fibula

tarsals

metatarsals

Observing

- Make a list of the joints in your body.
- Try to decide which sort each joint is.
- Make a sketch of each joint and mark on your sketch where the muscles seem to be fixed to the bone. (You can often find the end of the muscle because there is a strong band of stuff called tendon joining it to the bone. The Achilles tendon in your heel is a good example.)

EXTRAS

1 The photo shows an artificial hip joint. The ball fits into the socket on the pelvis. The sharp end of the joint is cemented into the thigh bone. Patients with artificial hips can usually walk three weeks after the operation.

(a) Why do people have artificial hips fitted?

(b) The artificial joint only lasts 5–10 years. Why is this?

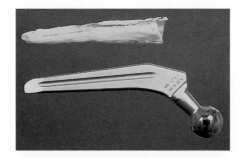

2 Most injuries in sport happen to knees and ankles. Why do you think this is?

3 Make a list of five joints in your body. For each joint, investigate the angle through which it can turn. If the joint turns in more than one direction, there will be more than one answer.

One important force is around us all the time. It is a force that stops things moving, or makes it hard for them to move. It is called *friction*.

You can feel the force of friction in these actions:
● Rub your hand on the bench. Press gently and then hard.

● Wave your hand in the air carefully. Do it slowly and then quickly.
● Rub your hands together gently and then hard.
● Write with a pen pressing lightly. Then press hard.

Slipping and sliding

Friction stops your shoes from sliding. Here are some things that decide if a shoe will slide or not:
– the type of sole
– the size of the sole
– the weight in the shoe

● Choose one of these things: sole type, sole size or shoe weight. Find out how changing it makes the shoe more or less likely to slide.

Hint: Here is *one* method of measuring the force needed to slide the shoe:

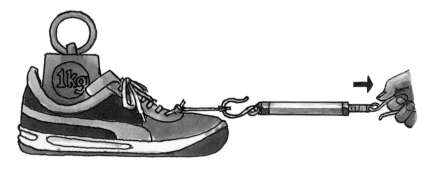

● Take care to alter only the thing you want to change. Everything else must be kept the same.

● Write up your results.
● If you have time, investigate another factor shown in the drawings.

● Get a piece of overhead projector transparency and some pens. Your group has to write an advert for a pair of non-slip, practical shoes for everyday use. Your advert should try to convince others in your class, with evidence, that the shoes are best.

1 Look at everyone else's adverts. Which group made the best job of convincing everybody which were the best shoes? Why?

A lot of friction

I was coiling my rope at the end of a super day's climbing when I heard a desperate shout from below me: 'Top rope, quick!'

A man soloing (climbing alone) up a route was in trouble. I had no time to think. I flung the end of my rope over the edge. With a desperate lunge, the soloer grabbed the rope, and hung from it by his hands. Nearly all his weight came on me; only the friction as the rope ran over the edge of the crag stopped me from being pulled over with him.

Now I had a problem. I couldn't pull him up – you try pulling 60kg up a cliff! So I had to lower him. Lowering is easiest if you run the rope through a descendeur. The friction between the descendeur and the rope controls the lowering. I hadn't time to arrange that. And the guy at the other end would only last a few seconds hanging from his arms. I had to lower him fast. I let the rope run out through my hands and round my waist. It went pretty fast, but even so it seemed to take ages until I heard a cry: 'He's down!'

I looked at my hands where the rope had been. They were agony. There were burn lines where the rope had slid as I lowered him. I can still see the scars now, six months later. He was OK, but I think the experience put him off soloing.

Communicating

2 How heavy was the soloer?
3 Why wasn't the writer pulled over the edge?
4 Explain, in your own words, how a descendeur helps with lowering.
5 The angle that the rope runs through a descendeur controls the speed of the rope. Which of these two climbers will go down faster? Why?
6 How did the writer get burned?

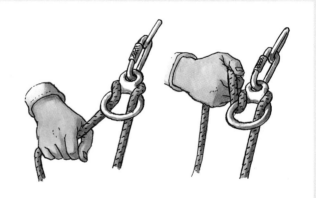

EXTRAS

Planning

1 Your skateboard wheels are rusty and they hardly turn. All you can find in the house that might help are margarine, cooking oil and soap. Write a plan for an investigation to find out which of these three things is best for getting the wheels moving well.

2 Lubricants are used to reduce friction. What effect do lubricants (like chalk, oil, and water) have on a surface? Plan an investigation. You could try using a shoe with weights in it on a piece of wood. If you tilt the wood, the shoe will slide. The more tilt you need to make the shoe slide, the greater the friction. Does the surface you use affect the results?

3 What is the best type of floor for a classroom? Why? How would you test your choice?

11·7 Using friction

Friction is a force that engineers usually try to make smaller. But there are times when friction is important.

Parachuting

Parachutes work because of friction between the parachute and the air. The more friction there is, the slower the parachute drops.

Investigating

- Design a parachute to carry a 10 gram payload from 2 metres high. It has to fall as slowly as possible. You will need to decide:
  - which material to make the canopy from
  - which material to use for the 'lines'
  - how to join the strings to the canopy and the payload to the strings
  - how to launch your parachute (you may not throw it).
- When your teacher has checked your design, make the parachute.
- Try it out and improve it so that it drops as slowly as possible.
- Time it and compare it with other groups' parachutes.
- Write up your design and results.
- If you can, find out how the mass of the payload affects the speed of dropping. Does 20 grams make the parachute fall twice as fast as 10 grams?
- Make a good display of your results.

Free fall

'I couldn't even do up my chinstrap, I was so nervous. The instructor opened the door and told me to kneel in the doorway. I knew my mother was right when she said I was mad. I couldn't even see the ground, it was so far away.

'Then the green light went on and the four of us were out of the back of the plane. I started spinning, but the training came in useful. I spread myself out into a star, and all at once I stopped spinning and started floating. The others caught me, and for a few seconds we gripped each other in a ring.

'All too soon they told me I had to pull the ripcord. There was the familiar jerk, and I was way above them and hardly moving. The landing was just routine. I'd done it!'

Reducing friction

A kingfisher in normal flight.

It sees a fish in the water and dives.

The kingfisher flies off with its catch.

Observing

● What do you notice about the bird? Draw sketches and describe why the bird's shape changes the way it does.

Streamlining

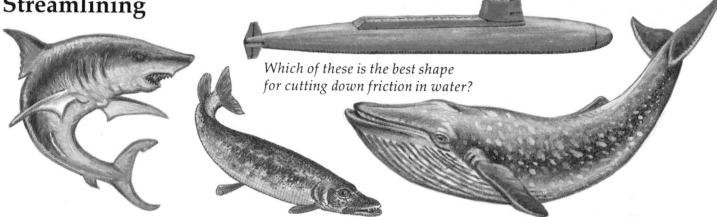

Which of these is the best shape for cutting down friction in water?

● Take some 20-gram lumps of Plasticine.
● Make each lump into a different streamlined shape.
● Find out how long it takes for each of these shapes to travel down a 1 metre tube of water.
● Put your results, with drawings, in your book.

● Use the tube of water to plan an investigation to answer *one* of these questions:
  – Does a heavy shape go faster than a light one?
  – How does the runniness of the liquid in the tube affect your results? (You can make the water thicker by adding a little wallpaper paste to it.)

EXTRAS

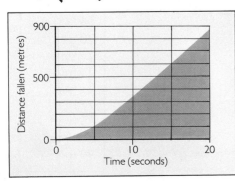

1 This graph shows you how far a free-fall parachutist travelled in the first 20 seconds after jumping.
(a) How far did she fall altogether?
(b) How far did she fall between:
(i) 0 and 5 seconds?
(ii) 5 and 10 seconds?
(iii) 10 and 15 seconds?

(iv) 15 and 20 seconds?
(c) Did she keep on getting faster?
(d) Can you think of a reason to explain your answer to (c)? (Hint: it is something to do with friction).

2 Craft that travel away from the Earth (e.g. satellites) are not streamlined. Why not?

11·8 Speed

How can you measure speed?

- Decide what you need to measure, then try to find out how fast some of these things go:
  - a person walking
  - a person running
  - a wind-up toy car
  - a maggot or woodlouse moving away from a light
  - a car on the road (take care!) ⚠

- Get your plan checked first.
- Write about what you did. Try to explain *why* you did it that way.

These sprinters are travelling at about 10 metres per second.

How fast?

- Match each object with the correct top speed:

33 m/s
14 000 m/s
20 m/s
2 mm/s
20 m/s
25 m/s
27 m/s
55 m/s
650 m/s
90 m/s

Speed traps

The police have a special radar to check that drivers are keeping to the speed limits. Many motorists complain about them, but they are there to keep the roads safe for everyone.

Radar uses a type of wave. These are rather like the waves that carry TV pictures, or the microwaves in a microwave oven.

The equipment contains a transmitter and a receiver. The radar wave is sent out from the transmitter. When it hits a metal object like a car, it bounces back to the receiver. The faster the car is moving, the more the wave is squashed up when it bounces back.

The receiver compares the wave sent out with the one that comes back. It contains a micro-processor that converts this information into a speed.

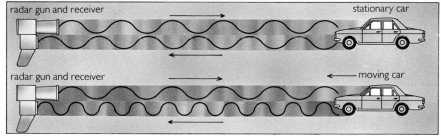

Changing speed

There are two ways of changing speed:
– *accelerating*: getting faster.
– *decelerating*: getting slower.

An instrument that measures changes in speed is called an *accelerometer*. Here is one type of accelerometer. The bigger the change in speed, the further the weight swings.

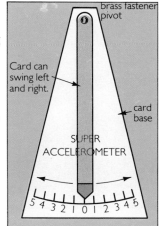

- Use the design to make your own accelerometer. You will need to think of a way to record the biggest distance that the weight swings. It will not stop at that point, but swing back again.
- Use your accelerometer to put these accelerations and decelerations in order:
  – starting to walk
  – starting to run
  – starting to sprint
  – a car pulling off (you need to be in the car)
  – bumping into someone when walking
  – stopping on a bike. (Get a friend to look at the accelerometer. Do NOT do it all yourself!)

EXTRAS

1 Try to work out the average speed for your journey to school. Think carefully what you will need to measure. A map and a watch may help you.

2 The faster you go, the harder it is to stop. Plan an investigation to find out how the distance you need to stop on a bike depends on the speed you are going at. *Don't* try your plan without an adult to supervise.

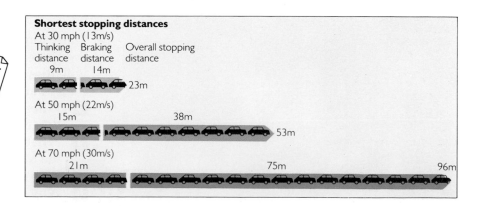

Shortest stopping distances

At 30 mph (13m/s)
Thinking distance 9m, Braking distance 14m, Overall stopping distance 23m

At 50 mph (22m/s)
15m, 38m, 53m

At 70 mph (30m/s)
21m, 75m, 96m

A Formula 1 margarine tub

How far can one rubber band push a margarine tub along the floor? You will need a 250g margarine tub as a car and a cut rubber band as a launcher.

- First make the launcher. You must not fix the band to the tub, and the tub must go along the floor.
- Test your launcher to make sure that it works.
- Investigate how far the tub goes if you pull the band back with different forces. You can use a newton meter to measure how much force you pull the band back with.
- Try at least five different forces.
- Plot a graph of force against the distance travelled.

1 How does the force on the tub affect the way it moves?

2 Would the tub go further if it weighed more?

- Plan and carry out an investigation to see what difference the mass of the tub makes to how far it goes.

Rockets

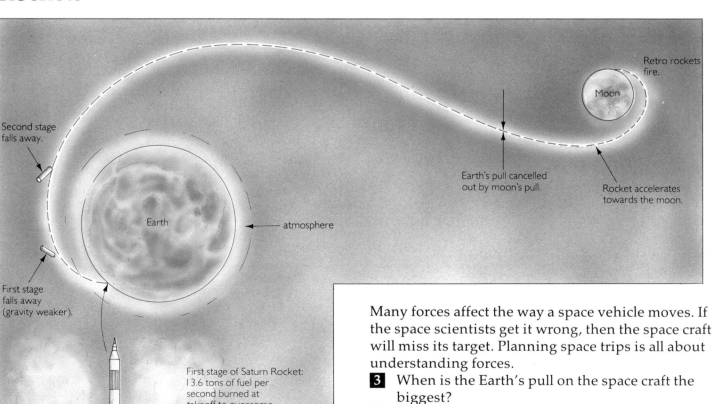

Second stage falls away.

First stage falls away (gravity weaker).

Earth

atmosphere

First stage of Saturn Rocket: 13.6 tons of fuel per second burned at takeoff to overcome gravity.

Earth's pull cancelled out by moon's pull.

Rocket accelerates towards the moon.

Moon

Retro rockets fire.

Many forces affect the way a space vehicle moves. If the space scientists get it wrong, then the space craft will miss its target. Planning space trips is all about understanding forces.

3 When is the Earth's pull on the space craft the biggest?

4 What makes the space craft accelerate towards the Moon?

5 Why does it need to fire retro-rockets?

6 Why does a Saturn rocket have three stages?

Cars

Model	Engine size (cm³)	Top speed (m/s)	Mass (kg)	Acceleration (time from 0 to 25 m/s) (seconds)
Rover				
213	1300	32	875	13.0
216	1600	34	925	10.9
820	2000	40	1250	9.7
Sterling	2500	43	1375	7.8
Ford Sierra				
1.6L	1600	34	980	12.0
1.8L	1800	35	1020	11.4
2.0LX	2000	38	1025	10.8
Vauxhall Cavalier				
1.3	1300	33	950	15.0
1.6	1600	34	1000	12.0
1.8	1800	38	1020	9.2
2.0CD (diesel)	2000	37	1035	8.7

Communicating

7 What is the engine size of a Ford Sierra 1.8L?
8 Which cars have a mass greater than 1200kg?
9 Which car has the best acceleration?
● Copy and fill in a table in your book like this:

1600 cm³ engine cars		
Name	Mass	Acceleration
Rover 216		

10 What does your table tell you about how a car's *mass* affects its *acceleration*?
● You have to make a car that will accelerate well. Make a list of things that the car should have.
● Design an advert for the Rover Sterling. The advert must show how it compares with the other makes of car. It must be clear and eye-catching.

EXTRAS

1 (a) What forces pull the people on this fairground ride?
(b) What would happen if the ride went at half speed? Why?
(c) Why don't people fall out when the ride is upside-down?

2 An MG Metro 6R4 is a saloon car with a very fast acceleration. It did 0–25m/s in 4.1 seconds in 1986. Why is this so much quicker than the Rover Sterling?

11:10 Bouncing forces

What makes a ball bounce?

- Choose four balls of about the same size that are different.
- Make a table like this one:

9/4/00 Comparing bounce				
Ball	Case	Inside: solid or air?	Mass (g)	Bounce
Golf Table-tennis	White plastic	Solid		

- Look at each ball in turn. Write down what the case is made of, and if the ball is solid or not.
- You will need to make some measurements to complete the table. Mass is easy, but think carefully how you will compare the bounce of each ball.
- When you have tested each ball, write down what you think makes a ball bouncy.

Does temperature matter?

Squash players always hit the ball around before they start a game.

1 What does this do to the ball? Why?

- Find out if bounciness is something to do with how hot the ball is. You can make the ball hotter by putting it into hot water. But you must let the ball reach the same temperature as the water.

Rubber is not a good conductor and the ball only warms up slowly.

- You must also think how you will measure bounciness.
- Do a display that shows how the ball's bounciness depends on its temperature. You may need to share some results with other groups to make a good display.

Does the surface matter?

Tennis is played on many types of surfaces: gravel, clay, tarmac, grass, plastic and wood are examples. The type of surface makes a big difference to the game. Surfaces with little bounce tend to favour players with a more powerful game. Slower surfaces give longer rallies and there is less volleying.

- Plan and carry out tests to put the surfaces used for playing tennis in order of bounciness.
- Find out which artificial surface could replace grass at Wimbledon.

2 What would be the advantages and disadvantages of not having to use grass courts?

Investigating

A ball launcher

- Your group has a challenge. You have to make a 'machine' that uses an elastic band to fire a table-tennis ball into a bucket two metres away. You can use these things:
    - a laboratory stand and clamp
    - an elastic band
    - a cardboard tube
    - some scrap card
    - some Sellotape
    - some brass paper fasteners
    - a table-tennis ball
    - some string or cotton
    - a stool

    Your machine will be judged on the best of five shots. The machine must have a device that fires it. You are not allowed just to pull the band back with your fingers.

    The problems seem to be:
    - how to make the launcher accurate
    - how to get the band to fire with the same strength each time.
    - how to make a trigger to fire it.

- Do a design with your friends. This sketch may give you some help, but don't rely on it.

- Test your design, then compare it with other groups' devices.
- When you have finished, do a good drawing of your final machine. Use labels on the design that show all the improvements you would make if you made another one.

EXTRAS

Planning

1 How does the bounciness of a football change with the amount of air in it? Do a plan for an investigation to find out.

2 Why does the air pressure in a car tyre get bigger during a long motorway journey?

3 Can you predict rebounds? When a snooker ball hits a cushion, or a football hits a wall, how does it bounce?
(a) Carry out an investigation to find out if you can predict the rebound if you know the approach angle.
(b) Does the rebound angle stay the same if the ball is hit at different speeds?
(c) Does the rebound angle stay the same if you hit the ball with spin?

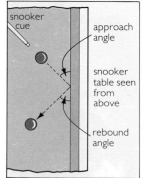

snooker cue

approach angle

snooker table seen from above

rebound angle

11·11 Changing the force – machines

A machine is a device that alters the size or direction of a force. Here are some everyday machines:

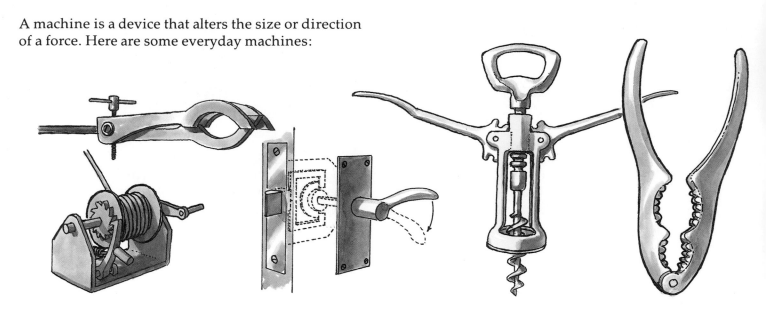

1 Which of these needs a small force from you to make or move a larger force?

2 Which of these change the direction of the force?

● Draw up a table like the one on the right. Fill it in for each machine.

● Then think of some other machines and add them to your table.

12/4/00 Machines			
What the machine does	Does it move a smaller or larger force than you use?	Does it change the direction of the force?	Which moves further: your hand or the load?

Gears

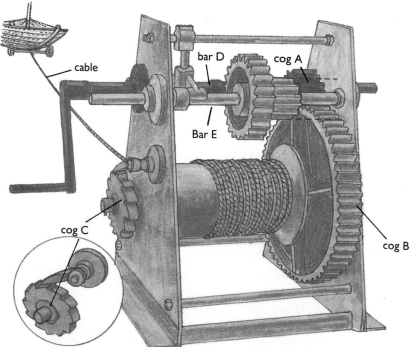

Some machines use gears. Gears change the speed, size or direction of a force. Look at this machine carefully, then answer the questions about it.

3 What do you think the machine is for?

4 Describe carefully what will happen when the handle is turned. A sketch may help you.

5 Why is cog A so small, and cog B so big?

6 What do you think cog C is for? (Look at the close-up of it.)

7 The handle will only turn one way. Is it clockwise or anticlockwise?

8 The machine can be altered by moving bar D to the left and bar E to the right. Why would anyone want to do this?

Investigating machines

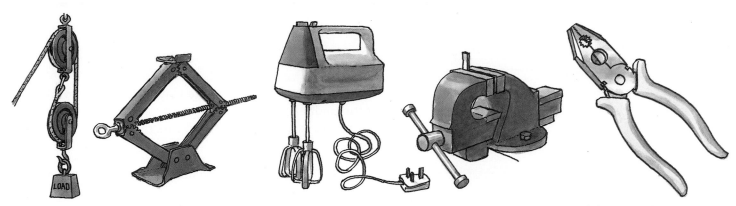

- Investigate some simple machines.
- For each machine, find out what it does and how it does it.

9 How far does the load move when the force you use moves 10cm?

10 How much force do you use to move the load?

(Put a load on the machine if there isn't one on it.)

11 Does the load move faster or slower than the force you apply?

12 Does the load move in the same direction as the force you use?

- Look at as many machines as you can.

Testing a machine

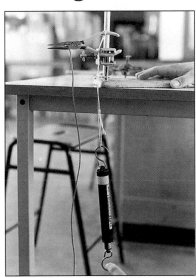

- Find out how much force is needed to do these jobs:
  - cut a piece of paper with scissors
  - cut thin card with the same scissors
  - cut wire insulation with pliers
  - cut wire with pliers

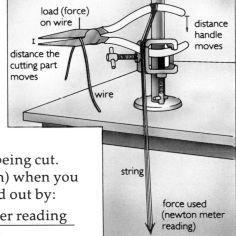

Here is one way of carrying out the tests:
- Try to work out the force on the thing being cut. Make the measurements shown (in mm) when you cut something. The force can be worked out by:

$$\frac{\text{distance handle moves} \times \text{newton meter reading}}{\text{distance cutting part moves}}$$

EXTRAS

1 Here are some gears in a car. Work out or find out the job of each of these machines in a car.

2 Stonehenge was built about 4000 years ago. The biggest stones came from Wales, over 150km away. Use sketches to show:

(**a**) how you think the stones were moved that far (they weigh as much as a medium-sized lorry).

(**b**) how you think they were lifted upright.

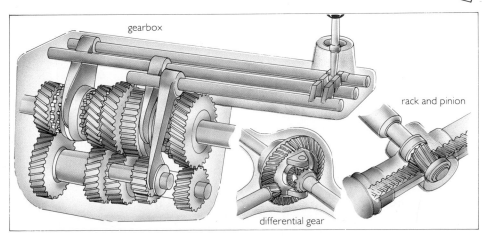

11·12 *Investigating bicycles*

Gears

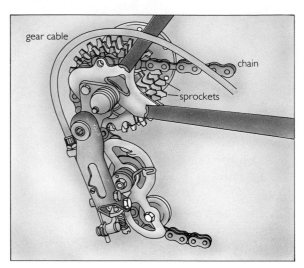

- Investigate the gears on a bike.
- Find out the distance that the bike travels for one complete turn of the pedals in each gear.
- Carry out an investigation to fill in this table:

Gear	Distance bike travels when pedals do one complete turn in this gear	No. of teeth on gear sprocket*
Biggest sprocket		
Next sprocket		
. . .		

*If your gears are inside the back axle, you will not be able to fill this in.

Bike friction

- Draw a good diagram of a bicycle on a piece of large paper. Do not use red or green in the drawing.
- On the drawing mark in green all the places where you want very little friction.
- Mark in red all the places where you need friction.

- Look at the places you have coloured green. Make a list of all the ways that friction is reduced in a bike.

- Look at all the places you have coloured red. Make a list of all the ways that friction is increased.

Bike grip

This investigation is about the best pressure for a bike tyre.

- You will need a bike, a pump that fits it, *either* some black paper and some chalk *or* some black powder paint and some white paper.
- Let down your front tyre gently.
- Chalk or paint the tyre in one place for about 20cm.

20 cm

- Place the chalked/painted tyre on the paper and carefully sit on the bike. Don't bounce – you may puncture the tyre.
- Put five pumfuls of air in the tyre and repeat the process.

- Make a tyre pattern on a clean piece of the paper.
- Label each pattern with the number of pumps of air in the tyre.

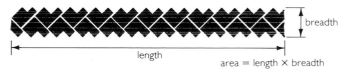

- Make an estimate of the area of the tyre touching the ground each time.
- Do this until the tyre is at full pressure.
- Plot a graph of area on the ground against pumfuls of air in the tyre.

2 What is the pattern in your results?
3 How does a flattish tyre help cycling?
4 What problems are there with having flattish tyres?

Brakes

Brakes are levers. In this investigation you can find out more about how they work. You will need to work with a friend to make the measurements.

Measuring pull

- Use two newton meters. Hook a strong meter around the brake block arm, and tie the other end with rope to a strong fixed point like a tree or post.
- Move the bike so that the rope is tight, but not pulling.
- With the other meter, pull on the brake lever. Do a gentle pull, and write down the readings on both meters.
- Then do a medium pull, and finally a hard pull.
- Make a chart from your results.

Measuring movement

- Remove the newton meters.
- Carry out tests to fill in this table:

Pull on lever:	Gentle	Medium	Hard
How far end of brake lever moved:			
How far brake block moved:			

5 What do these two investigations tell you?

- Use a similar method to find out if side-pull brakes are as powerful as centre-pull brakes.

Side-pull brakes   Centre-pull brakes

EXTRAS

1 Mountain bikes are designed to go over very rough ground, and up very steep hills. Draw an outline of a mountain bike. Use labels with notes to show all the features that you think a mountain bike should have.

2 (a) Write a 'Safety audit' for a bicycle on one side of a piece of paper. It should say how you would check that a bike is safe to ride.
(b) Write a safety system for cyclists on one side of a piece of paper. It should say what you need to do to ride a bike safely on the road.

12 INVESTIGATIONS

12·1 Out of this world

This is what our world looks like from space. You can see the Earth outlined against the sun on a background of stars. Our sun is a star, because it produces its own light. The sun, the Earth and the planets are all part of our solar system.

The universe

The Earth is a tiny part of the universe. Imagine taking the same picture from a star outside the solar system. The sun would look like a rather faint point of light, but you would not see the Earth at all. It is too small, and does not produce its own light.

Most astronomers think that the universe started with a big explosion 15 000 million years ago. Ever since, it has been spreading out. The universe is a bit like a balloon being blown up bigger and bigger. And the solar system is only a tiny dot just under the balloon's skin.

Our planets

How the nearest planets in our solar system compare with the Earth

Planet	Distance from sun	Diameter of planet	Mass of planet	Time to go round the sun
		(all compared to the Earth)		
Earth	1.0	1.0	1.0	1 year
Mercury	0.4	0.4	0.06	0.2 years
Venus	0.7	1.0	0.8	0.6 years
Mars	1.5	0.5	0.1	1.9 years
Jupiter	5.2	11.2	317.0	11.9 years
Saturn	9.5	9.5	95.0	29.5 years

The Earth is 150 million kilometres from the sun. Its diameter is 13 000km. Its mass is 6 million million million million kilograms.

- With your friends, make a display of the sun and the six nearest planets. Use 1cm as the size of the Earth. Draw and cut out a circle that is the right size for each planet.

- Make a solar system display from your cut-outs. Draw the sun at one end of your poster. Put the Earth on the poster 5cm from the sun. Stick the other planets on the poster in the right places.

- The sun is 110 times bigger than the Earth. Make a scale model of the sun for your display.

The planet Jupiter and two of its moons, photographed by Voyager 1 in 1979 from 28.4 million kilometres away.

The planet Saturn photographed by Voyager 2 in 1981 from 21 million kilometres away.

Summer and winter

The Earth takes just over 365 days to go once round the sun. As the Earth turns, it is tilted on its axis.

In summer the sun's rays fall almost directly on Britain. This makes the sun feel hot. In winter, the northern half of the Earth is tilted away from the sun. The sun's rays are spread over a wider area, so it is not so warm.

The table below shows how high the sun gets at noon in London (when you can see it!). A metre ruler was put in the ground. The measurements show the shadow made by the ruler.

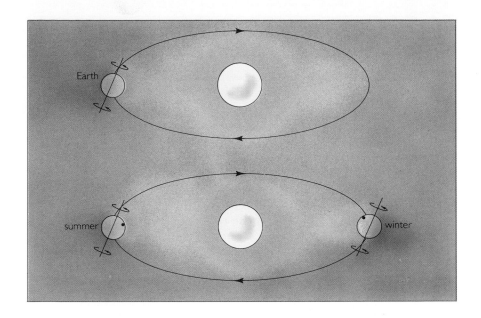

Month:	Jan	Feb	Mar	Apr	May	June	Jul	Aug	Sept	Oct	Nov	Dec
Shadow length (cm)	365	260	144	100	75	62	75	100	144	260	365	430

- Do a display graph of these shadows.
- Explain the shape of the graph.

Day and night

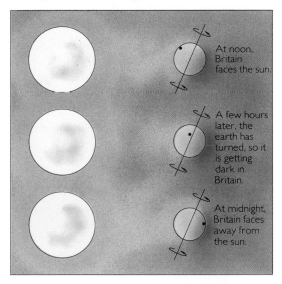

At noon, Britain faces the sun.

A few hours later, the earth has turned, so it is getting dark in Britain.

At midnight, Britain faces away from the sun.

The Earth does not just go round the sun. It spins on its axis as well. It takes 24 hours to do one complete turn. This gives us days and nights.

- On a sunny day, put a metre ruler or stick in the ground. As near as possible every hour, measure the shadow the stick makes.
- Make a display of your results.
- Explain the shape of your display.

We can use sundials to tell the time.

- Design a *portable* sundial that you could carry like a watch. Think hard! Sundials have to face the right way to show the time (and they need some sun, but that's another problem).

EXTRAS

1 There are three other planets in our solar system. Here is a little information about them (compared to the Earth again):

	Size	Distance from sun
Uranus	3.9	19
Neptune	4.0	30
Pluto	0.3	39

Add these to your solar system poster. You may need more paper!

2 Choose one planet. What equipment would you need to live there? Describe what you think it would be like to spend a day and a night on the planet.

The Moon's diameter is about one-quarter of the Earth's. Add the Moon to your display. Find out:
(**a**) how the Moon causes eclipses (when the sun is blotted out on Earth),
(**b**) what the Moon's phases are, and what causes them.

Making soil

Soil does not just happen. It is made when rocks get worn away by ice, wind and rain. Over millions of years, rocks are broken up into tiny particles. Plant roots also help to break rocks up.

Some of the rock particles are carried in streams and rivers, particularly during floods. When the river runs more slowly, the particles sink and form mud. If the river or sea dries up, or the land rises, soil is left.

As animals and plants die, they decay into the soil. Microbes and fungi live in the soil. They help to rot the dead plants, making humus. Humus is what a poor soil needs to become a good growing soil. Worms break up the soil and mix in the humus. They help soils to drain, and let air get in.

Layers of one type of soil. The dark top layer is rich in decayed matter from plants and animals.

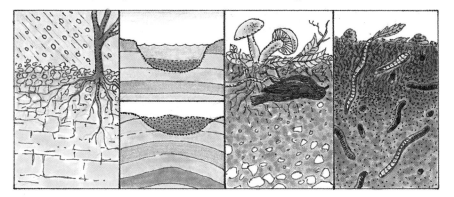

Types of soil

Soils can be very different.

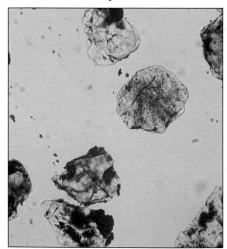

Sandy soil has large air spaces. It does not hold water well and is usually dry. It is called a *light* soil. Light soils can be improved by adding compost or manure.

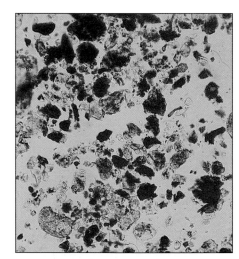

Loam soil has a mixture of particles. It holds water well, but does not get water-logged easily. It usually contains plenty of humus.

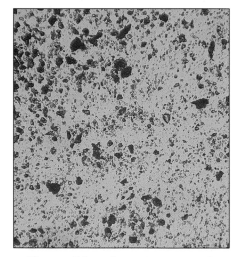

Clay soil has few air spaces. It holds water, but does not drain well. It is called a *heavy* soil – you will know why if you have tried to dig it! Heavy soils can be improved by adding lime or manure.

Testing soil

- Test some samples of soil of your own. The samples need to be fresh, and you must break up any lumps that you see.
- Write a report on each soil that you test.

- Find out how much humus is in the soil. Use 100g of dry soil. Heat it in a tin tray with a Bunsen for 15 minutes; stir it carefully while you heat. The heat should burn off the humus, leaving a light ash. Re-weigh it when it is cool.

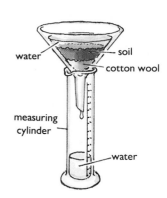

- Find out the type and size of particle in the soil. Crush the soil with a pestle and mortar, then look at a few grains with a microscope.

- Find out how much air is in 50cm^3 of crushed, dry soil. One way to do this is to mix the soil thoroughly with 50cm^3 of water. 50 + 50 should make 100, but they will make less than this if there is air in the soil. The difference between what you get and 100 is the amount of air in the soil.

water

soil

- Find out how well the soil drains. Think carefully how you can make this a fair test of each soil. It is best to crush the soil and to wet it before making any measurements.

water — soil
cotton wool
measuring cylinder
water

water + indicator
soil

- Find out whether the soil is acid or alkaline. Shake it with some distilled water, then let it stand until it clears. This may take some time! Test the clear liquid with Universal Indicator solution.

- Find out what happens when you shake a little of the soil with water in a gas jar. Put a few cubic centimetres of crushed soil into the jar. Add about four times as much water. Shake the mixture hard, but take care not to spill it. Let the soil settle, then note what you see.

humus and froth

clear water

fine light particles

darker bigger bits

small stones

- Find out how quickly the soil dries out. Again you will need to think how you can compare the soils fairly. An oven at about 60°C will speed up the tests.

EXTRAS

1 Plan and carry out an investigation to see how well seeds grow in sandy, clay and loam soils. You should compare several seeds in each soil, not just one. (Why?)

2 (a) What stops soil from being blown away?
(b) In many parts of the world, trees and hedges are being pulled up or cut down. This is bad for the soil. Why?

3 (a) Find out how a worm lives: how it moves, feeds and reproduces.
(b) Look at a worm from your garden. Has it got a head and a tail? Eyes? Mouth? Do a good drawing of it, then return it to the garden.

Everything needs somewhere to live. Plants grow best in places that suit them. Animals live in places that are safe and provide them with food.

Looking at habitats

A *habitat* is the area where something lives.

● Choose a patch of ground near your school or home that is likely to have some living things in it. An area about 4 metres by 5 metres is plenty. Try to include some different types of terrain in your patch: dry, damp, sunny, grassy, concrete or tarmac.

   Try these activities, but take care not to pick or damage any living things.

● Make a sketch-plan of your patch. Use 5cm to represent 1m. Mark on it the types of terrain in your area.

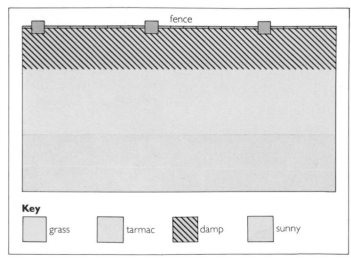

Key

grass   tarmac   damp   sunny

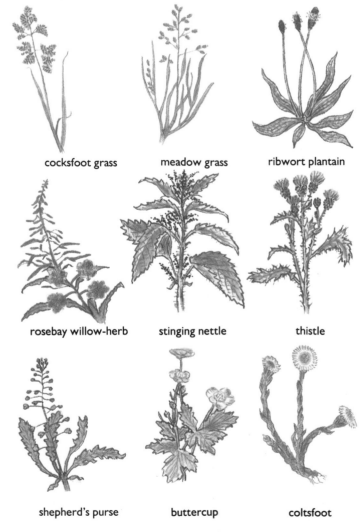

cocksfoot grass   meadow grass   ribwort plantain

rosebay willow-herb   stinging nettle   thistle

shepherd's purse   buttercup   coltsfoot

● Do a survey of the flora (plants) in your patch. Identify as many different plants as you can. If you find things that you cannot identify, do a sketch and look up the plant later in a reference book.

If there are too many things growing in your patch, you can do a survey by looking at a small area only – say ½ metre by ½ metre.

- Do a survey of the fauna (animals) in your patch .
  Try to sketch what you find and note where you find it.

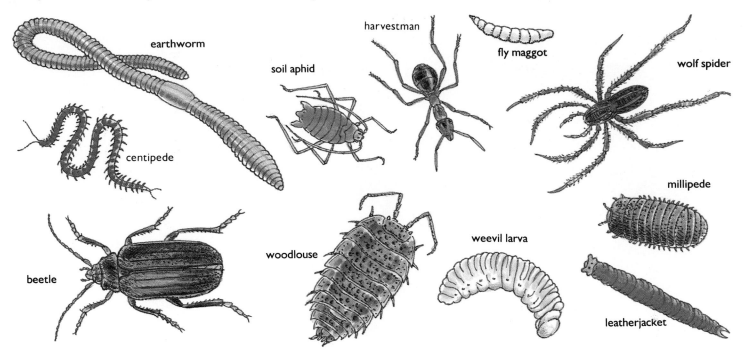

earthworm

harvestman

fly maggot

soil aphid

wolf spider

centipede

millipede

beetle

woodlouse

weevil larva

leatherjacket

1 Is there a pattern in the way that the plants have grown in your patch? Where have they grown best? Where have things not grown well? Can you explain this?

2 Are there any signs of human activity in your patch? What are they? Where have they come from? How have they affected the flora and fauna?

3 Where do the animals like to live? Why?

- Choose a plant and an animal that are common in your patch. Find a way of estimating how many of each are in the patch.

  All the plants and animals that live in a particular area make up a *community*. The things in a community depend on each other for life.

- Make a chart that shows what feeds on what in your patch. You may need to guess in some cases. The chart is called a *food web*.

Water communities ⚠

You need a small brook or stream to try these investigations. Warning! Do not choose somewhere with deep or fast water that may be dangerous. Always work with a friend. Here are some activities to try:

- Make a scale drawing of a cross-section of the stream at one point. You will need to measure its width and its depth every 10cm or so across.
- Find a way of measuring how fast the stream flows, in metres per second.

- Find a way of measuring how much sediment is carried in the stream. Sediment is the solid particles carried by the water.
- Find out how polluted the water is. How acid is it? Is it clear or murky? What sort of things live in it?
- Find out how plants that live in the water compare with plants on the bank.

EXTRAS

1 Choose one animal or plant. Make a full-page report on it. Include drawings or photos, what sort of habitat it needs, what food and conditions it needs, and how it changes during its life.

2 Litter is a problem in many areas. Do a survey of litter in your street. Make a list of all the litter. Try to say where it came from and how long it will last. If you can, clean it up. Can you think of a way of keeping your street free of litter?

At the scene of the crime

'Now, Mrs Marshall, can we go over the missing items again? The burglar took:
– your cheque book and cheque card,
– a gold bracelet,
– a gold-plated fountain pen,
– about £50 in cash.

And you think that some of your whisky was drunk from this glass. We'll get the forensic team to check that over.'

REPORT

Date: 21/5/00

Incident: Burglary

Location: 35 Lowerwood Road, Matlock

Date/time of incident: 20/5/00, about 1.00 a.m.

Incident report: The intruder appears to have broken a window at the rear of the premises and entered through it. Several fabric fibres were left on the sharp edge of the frame. There was no apparent damage in the house, but we have taken a glass away for finger-printing.

Sample fingerprints:

The evidence

Some days later, a man was arrested trying to cash one of the stolen cheques. Before the case can go to court, the police have to prove that he was the man who had broken into Mrs Marshall's house. What have they got to go on?

Here are some ideas you can try:

Fibres

Find as many differences and similarities as you can between fibres from different materials. Try these tests:
- **Microscope:** For each fibre, estimate its size, colour and how it is made.
- **Burning:** Hold the fibre in tongs over a heatproof mat. Light one end and see how the rest burns. Does it leave ash?
- **Stretch:** How much does the fibre stretch with a weight on it? How much force is needed to break it?

- The suspect was wearing a wool jumper when he was arrested. Could you match one of the fibres from the scene of the crime with one from his jumper?

Cotton

Wool

Nylon

Ink

The suspect said that a gold-plated pen found on him was his and not Mrs Marshall's. Fortunately, Mrs Marshall used a special sort of ink. Using a technique called chromatography, the forensic team tried to match the ink in the pen with Mrs Marshall's ink.

● Try this technique:

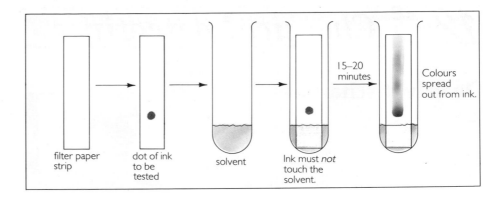

filter paper strip — dot of ink to be tested — solvent — Ink must *not* touch the solvent. — 15–20 minutes — Colours spread out from ink.

Fingerprinting

Here are three ways of getting good fingerprints:

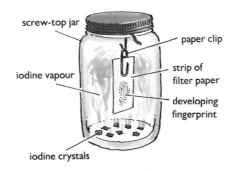

screw-top jar
paper clip
iodine vapour
strip of filter paper
developing fingerprint
iodine crystals

● Press your finger gently on a clean sheet of glossy paper.
● Sprinkle some fine powder on the print (try carbon powder or aluminium powder).
● Use a fine brush to brush some of the powder off. You should have a print left.

● Make a fingerprint on a small piece of rough paper.
● Ask your teacher to hang the paper in a jar of iodine. (**Warning:** iodine vapour is toxic.) ⚠
● Leave it for 30 minutes.

● Rub coloured chalk over one of your fingers.
● Gently press and roll the finger onto the sticky side of a piece of Sellotape. This is a good way of making a set of your own prints to stick in your book.

There are three main types of fingerprint:

Arch

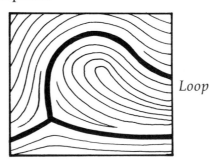
Loop

Whorl

● Find out which types of print you and your friends have.
● Find out if the prints from each of your fingers and thumbs are the same.
● Find out if toes make prints. Are these prints the same as your fingers?

EXTRAS

1 A perfectly good fingerprint found at the scene of a crime can be useless. Think of as many reasons as you can why this might be.

2 Can you tell age from fingerprints? Look at the fingerprints of people of different ages and see if you can spot any differences.

3 Use chromatography to find out what dyes are used to colour your felt pens. You can use blotting paper with water as a solvent.

12:5 Chemical detectives

Deadly discharge

The warning buzzer on the automatic analyser sounded. Ben quickly checked the readings. Most of them seemed normal, until he got to the heavy metal levels. These were well over the danger limit and had tripped the alarm. Now Ben had to sort out where the effluent was coming from, and he had to act fast. Heavy metal effluent would kill all the life in the river.

'It must be coming in between Mere Bank and Bowerleaze, or I'd have heard from Dave at the next monitoring point,' thought Ben. 'Who've we got in that stretch?' He checked the map and picked up the phone. 'Is that TopChem?' asked Ben. 'Lark and Swallow Water here. Can I talk to Dr Baker?'

'Someone's discharging effluent into the Lark, and it could be you,' said Ben.

'Do you know what it is?' asked Dr Baker.

'Not yet,' said Ben, 'but it's likely to kill many fish. Please check your output today and let me know. Oh, and send me today's output samples.'

'OK,' said Dr Baker.

Ben said the same thing to the other factory managers on his stretch of the river. His next problem was to decide which factory's samples contain the effluent. Could you help him?

Testing chemicals ⚠️ 🥽

Nowadays there are machines that will identify the chemicals in a sample of water quickly and accurately. They are so sensitive that they can often detect 1 or 2 parts of chemical in a million parts of water.

Compounds

Most chemicals that are tested are *compounds*. A compound is two or more elements (see 10.1) joined together.

There are some simple tests that you can do to identify chemical compounds.
- Find the chemicals in some of these substances using the tests on the next page:
  - eggshell
  - stomach powder
  - limestone
  - chalk
  - salt
  - washing soda
  - baking powder
  - fertiliser

Minerals

You could also test some *minerals*. Minerals are chemicals that are found in the Earth. Some minerals are precious crystals, like emerald or amethyst. Others are metal ores, like haematite (iron ore) and galena (lead ore).
- Investigate:
  - gypsum
  - halite

- malachite   - calcite   - fluorite

Chemical tests

These tests only identify a few chemicals. There are lots of others, and there are many other tests. If you do not get a clear answer for a substance, be prepared to write 'I do not know, but it could be . . .'

Warning: Some of these tests involve acids. Be careful; use eye protection.

Tests for metals

Many tests do not give a clear answer. But if you put several results together, you can often make a good guess.

● Use your results to make a key to identify metals.

	Test	Comments
Solubility:	Put a little of the substance in a test tube. Add water and shake.	Most compounds of potassium and sodium are soluble in water. (But so are many other compounds.)
Colour:	Look at the compound or the solution it makes.	Blue: maybe copper. Green or brown: maybe iron. Clear solution: maybe sodium, potassium, magnesium.
Flame test:	Clean a nichrome wire in a hot Bunsen flame. Dip it in some dilute hydrochloric acid, then in some crushed substance. Put the wire in the flame, and look for any colour *straight away*. (Over 5 seconds is too long.)	Pink/lilac: potassium. Orange (persists): sodium. Red (faint): calcium. Green/blue: copper. Light green: barium. Crimson: strontium. White flashes (hard to see): lead.
Alkali test:	One extra test for metals is to add an alkali, like sodium hydroxide, to the substance. You can test this out. Dissolve some metal nitrates in a little water (not more than 1 cm deep). (Try sodium, calcium, copper, zinc, ammonium, aluminium). Add one or two drops of sodium hydroxide to each in turn and shake. Note what you see or smell. Then add 2 or 3cm more of sodium hydroxide and shake.	

Tests for other chemicals

	Test	Comments
Chloride:	Dissolve a little of the substance in water. If water will not work, use dilute nitric acid instead. Add one or two drops of dilute silver nitrate. (This is very expensive, so do not waste it!)	A chloride will go cloudy or white.
Sulphate:	Dissolve a little of the substance in water. If water will not work, use dilute hydrochloric acid. Add one or two drops of barium chloride. (**Caution: poison.**)	A sulphate will go white.
Carbonate:	Add one or two drops of dilute hydrochloric acid to the substance. If there is a fizz, crush some of the substance and put it in a test tube. Put 1cm of limewater in another tube. Add 1cm of dilute hydrochloric acid to the substance. Let the gas run into the limewater test tube for a minute. Shake the limewater tube. Carbon dioxide turns limewater cloudy. If the limewater goes cloudy, your substance contains a carbonate.	All carbonates fizz if you add acid. The gas is carbon dioxide. Carbon dioxide turns limewater cloudy. If the limewater goes cloudy, your substance contains a carbonate.

EXTRAS

Make a computer or visual key for metals using all the information on this page. Your first box could be 'What colour is the substance?' and it would lead to other boxes that give you more tests or answers.

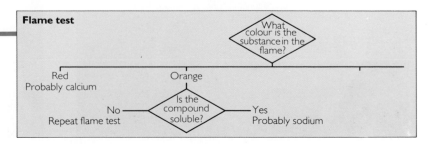

12·6 Zoos

What are zoos for?

Learning about animals

We can learn about how animals behave by watching them closely. To do this we need to make the zoo as much like their natural home as possible. Some animals help scientific research; armadillos grow leprosy microbes without getting ill. They are used to test drugs.

Protecting threatened species

Humans have almost wiped out some animals and destroyed the habitats of others. A zoo is one place where rare animals can be protected and bred. The Arabian oryx had become almost extinct, but was bred successfully in a zoo. It has now been re-introduced into its natural habitat.

Leisure

Many people go to the zoo simply for a day out. It is interesting to be able to see animals that in the wild live thousands of miles away.

Using a zoo

You will learn a lot more from a trip to the zoo if you decide to study just one thing. It could be one animal, or one feature (like ears or feeding or habitats) for several animals. Below are some ideas to help you.

Habitats

* How well has the zoo copied the animal's natural habitat?
* How are animals kept separate from people?
* Do all animals have a place where they can be on their own?
* What is provided to keep the animals happy?
* What climate does the animal need? How does the zoo provide it?

Feeding

* What food does the zoo need to provide?
* How often are different animals fed?
* Why are visitors not allowed to feed the animals?
* Why do animals' teeth stay healthy?

Breeding

* How often do certain animals breed each year?
* Do they lay eggs?
* How many babies are produced in each litter?
* How long does it take for the baby animal to become an adult?

Senses

● Make a chart of eye size, colour and position for some different animals.
  * What decides what an animal's eyes are like?
  * Which animals have the best sight?
● Make a set of sketches of animal ears.
  * Are any animals deaf?
  * Do all animals have two ears?
  * Which type of animals have the best hearing?

Moving

* How do the animals move? How many different ways of moving can you find in the zoo?
* How fast can different animals move?
* Why does each animal need to move?
* Do longer-legged animals go faster than short-legged ones?
* Does the zoo let the animals move like they would in the wild?

Defence

* What different methods do animals use to protect themselves? (There are many methods, so look carefully.)
* Which animals do not need to protect themselves? Why?
* Which animals have to defend themselves against their own species? Why?

EXTRAS

1 Is the guide to the zoo good? Re-write the bits you think are poor (or make a new guide). The zoo manager might be interested in your ideas.

2 Choose a tame animal that you can watch easily. A pet or even a human baby is ideal. Make a factfile for the animal. This should include things like:
– How and when it feeds.
– What it eats.

– When it is most active.
– When it sleeps.
– How it keeps warm.
– How it is looked after (and by whom).
– How it attracts attention.
– How it can be 'trained'.

135

12·7 Bread science

Making bread

Bread is mostly holes. How do they get there? Where do they come from?
- Make some bread and find out. If you use clean hands and equipment, you can eat the bread you make. Wear something to protect your clothes!

Ingredients

100g of plain flour
4g of fresh yeast (2g of dried yeast)
2g of sugar
1 pinch salt
20cm³ warm (not hot) water
a little spare flour

Method

- Put the yeast and sugar in a clean bowl with some of the water. Mix. Leave until it froths. If it does not froth, your yeast is not alive.

- Put the flour and salt in a mixing bowl. Make sure your hands are clean.

- Pour the yeast into the middle of the flour. Sprinkle some flour over the top. Leave for a few minutes.

- Add the rest of the water. Mix the flour and yeast to make *dough*. Once the yeast is mixed in, it is best to do the mixing in your hands. The more you squeeze and squash the dough, the better your bread should be.

- The dough should be soft, smooth and not sticky. If it is too dry, add a little water. If it is too sticky, dust your hands with flour.

- Make the dough into small rolls and leave them for an hour in a warm place.

- Heat an oven to gas mark 6 (200°C). Put the rolls on a baking tray and into the oven when it is hot. They will take 10 to 15 minutes to cook (more for bigger rolls).
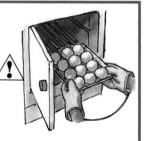

Jobs to do while your bread is rising or cooking

- Work out what your bread costs to make. Approximate costs per 100 grams: flour and sugar 5p, yeast 20p. 15 minutes of gas costs about 2p.

1 If you were a bakery manager, how much would you sell your rolls for? Explain your answer.

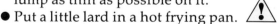

Oven fuel 1%
Wrapping 2%
Shop costs and profit 31%
Getting bread from factory to shop 15%
Ingredients 35%
Factory profit 4%
Other factory costs 12%

- Look at this loaf of bread. It shows how the price of a loaf is shared between all the people who make and sell it. Draw a similar 'loaf' that shows the price of your rolls.

2 Is your loaf cheaper or dearer? Why?

Testing yeast

This equipment can be used to measure how active yeast is.

The number of bubbles in a minute shows how well the yeast is working.

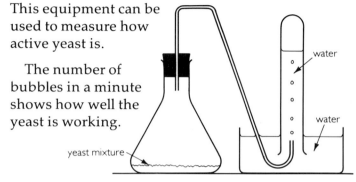

water

water

yeast mixture

- Test the equipment with the mixture you used to make bread (4g yeast, 2g sugar and a little warm water). The yeast takes a little while to get started, so leave the flask for 5 minutes.

- Then count the bubbles that it makes in the next minute. You will work faster on the investigations below if you share the work with other groups.

- Find out what happens if you make the yeast warmer or colder. You can do this by standing the flask in iced water or boiling water or warm water.

- Find out what happens if you use different amounts of sugar in the flask (try between 0 and 20 grams).

- Find out which gas yeast produces. Collect a test-tube full, then look at 10.10 for tests.

Making chapattis

Bread can be made without yeast. Here is a recipe for chapattis:
- Mix 100g of flour with ½ teaspoon of salt.
- Add water and mix in until you have a smooth dough.
- Squeeze the mixture for 15 minutes, then leave it for half an hour.
- Break it into 3cm lumps.
- Sprinkle some flour on a board, and roll each

lump as thin as possible on it.
- Put a little lard in a hot frying pan.
- Cook one slice at a time until you see bubbles in it. Then turn it over and cook till it is brown.

3 Where do the bubbles in chapattis come from?
4 The bubbles go as the chapatis cool down. Why? (It is easier to answer this question if you make some; they are particularly good with curry.)

EXTRAS

1 Yeast is also used to make alcohol. Find out how beer or wine is made. Why does bread not have alcohol in it?

2 Make some clinker toffee – but get an adult to help you with it.

Put 100g of sugar and 100g of syrup in a saucepan. Heat the pan gently. Add a pinch of salt and let the mixture boil. **Take care:** it will be *very* hot.

Use a wooden spoon to pick up a bit of the mixture and drop it into a dish of cold water. If the mixture goes hard, stop heating. If not, heat it some more, then test it again.

Stir in a level teaspoon of bicarbonate of soda. Then pour

the mixture on to a flat, greased baking tray. Let the clinker toffee cool, then eat a small piece.

Don't forget to wash up the things you used! Work out:
(**a**) why there are holes in the toffee,
(**b**) what it costs to make,
(**c**) what you should sell it for if you were in business.

12·8 Cleaning off grease

Oven dirt

Oven dirt is tough. It is made from food grease that has been burnt on to the sides of the oven. This makes it really hard to get rid of. A good oven cleaner dissolves the grease and makes it easy to wipe off.

Which substances will dissolve grease?

You need a *solvent* (something that dissolves other things).
● Plan some tests and get them approved first.
● Test as many solvents as you can, to see which can remove grease.

● When you have found two or three that work, do some careful tests. Take great care with solvents that are flammable or acid or alkali.
● First you need a standard greasy plate. You could make one by putting some grease on an ovenproof plate, then heating it in an oven for half an hour. You may have a better idea.

● Then you need to decide on a standard test:

– Should the plate be hot or cold?

– Will you soak it first?

– How much solvent will you use?

– What will you put the solvent on with?

– Will you scrub the plate?

– How long will you clean it for?

– How will you decide which solvent works best?

● Carry out your tests.
● Write a report on your findings.

Which? oven cleaner

The Consumers' Association is a group that helps people to choose what to buy. It tests things and recommends the ones that are the best value for money. Here is a part of their report on personal stereos.

	target price £	weight (see key)	features (see key)	in use	cassette replay classical	cassette replay pop
Aiwa HS-PO5 MkII (Japan)	55	I	abcdh	□	■	■
Alba PC6/PC8 (Japan)	10	II	ad	[14]	□	□
Boots PS22 (Japan)	13	I	d	◪	◪	□
Grundig Beat Boy 120 [11] (Japan)	25	I	abdhk	□	□	□
Matsui 6110 [18] (Japan)	13	I	d	◪	◪	□
Panasonic RQ-J50 [11] (Japan)	26	II	abd	◪	◪	□
Panasonic RQ-J60 (Japan)	25	I	abd	◪	◪	◪
Philips D6645 (Japan)	32	II	b[1]defh[6]	□	□	□
Sansui FXW30R [20] (Taiwan)	20	II	b[1]defh	◪		
Sony Walkman WM22 (Japan)	30	I	abdk	□	□	□
Sony Walkman WM24 (Japan)	40	I	abdhkt	□	□	□

Key to weight
I = up to 300g
II = 300g to 400g
III = 400g to 500g

KEY TO RATINGS

■ ◪ □ ◪ ■
best ←——→ worst

[1] Rewind by using manual reverse then forward wind
[2] Graphic equaliser
[3] CP16 (£25) is similar but also has AM radio
[4] FM only
[5] Tested as 3T24 (now discontinued), which has balance control
[6] Cue only
[7] From Currys. Now discontinued; may still be in shops
[8] From Tandy shops
[9] Includes cost of headphones which are an extra
[10] From Dixons
[11] Discontinued; may still be in shops
[12] Tested as KT4015 (now discontinued); cosmetic differences
[13] Tested as Triumph PH1205 (now discontinued); cosmetic differences
[14] Test result not available
[15] Tested as CS11
[16] Discontinued, may still be in shops; replaced by 3T33 (£19)
[17] Discontinued; may still be in shops. Turner pack available as extra (£30)
[18] From Currys
[19] Philips D6632 (£20) is smaller
[20] Discontinued; may still be in shops. Replaced by smaller FXW31R

Key to features

a = autostop at end of play
b = locking rewind
c = autostop at end of wind
d = locking fast forward wind
e = manual reverse play
f = auto reverse play
g = recording from radio and built-in microphone
h = cue and review
k = equalisation switch
m = separate left and right volume controls
n = balance control
p = tone control
t = Dolby B noise reduction
v = socket for second pair of headphones

BEST BUYS

 OVER £40 The **Aiwa HS-PO5 MkII** (£55), which has the best performance of all the sets on cassette

 UP TO £40 The **Grundig Beat Boy 120** (£25), and **Philips D6645** (£32)

UP TO £20 The **Alba PC6/PC8** (£10), **Boots PS22** (£13), **Crown CS55** (£13), **Ferguson 3T23** (£20), **Harvard PS75** (£10), **Matsui 6110** (£13) and the **Sansui FXW30R** (£20)

- Your job is to test some oven cleaners and to recommend a 'best buy'. Here are some ideas to help you, but you may think of others.

  – Is it easy to use?
  – Is it pleasant to use?
  – Is it corrosive? (Find out if it is acid or alkaline.)
  – Does it make any nasty fumes?
  – Could it damage anything (hands, wood or chrome, the ozone layer)?
  – What does it cost?
  – How many times can it be used?
  – Does it have any special features?
  – How well does it work?

- Plan some tests. You *must* get them approved first.

- When you have tested as many cleaners as you can, you have to produce a report. Before you start, think carefully how you will present all the information. At the end of the report, recommend a 'best buy'.

EXTRAS

1 Like ovens, some people have problems with grease. Many garage workers have permanently messy hands.
(**a**) How would hand cleaners need to be different from oven cleaners?
(**b**) Which type of cleaner (hand or oven) is more expensive? Why?

2(**a**) Microwave ovens do not get greasy like normal ovens. Why not?
(**b**) What would you recommend for cleaning a microwave oven? Why?

3 Why do we bother to clean ovens at all?

Circuits

In your first circuits you used torch bulbs joined with wires. Modern electrical equipment uses the same basic ideas. But if you look inside a computer there are not many wires or torch bulbs. The wires and bulbs have been replaced by electronic devices like transistors, chips and light-emitting diodes.

Transistors and chips are examples of *semi-conductors*. They are made from special crystals like silicon. Transistors work because they only conduct electricity in the right conditions. They are useful because they can turn on and off very fast, and they need very little electricity.

An electronic light

- You can make electronic circuits with wires like the circuits you made before. The difficulty is that the contacts are poor, and sometimes things do not work. It is far better to *solder* the components.

Here is a simple circuit to operate a light-emitting diode (LED).

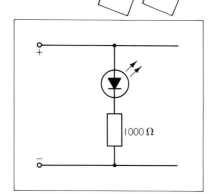

This design shows the same circuit soldered on matrix board. The board is cheap and can be re-used.

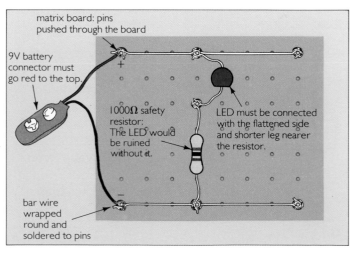

matrix board: pins pushed through the board

9V battery connector must go red to the top.

1000Ω safety resistor: The LED would be ruined without it.

LED must be connected with the flattened side and shorter leg nearer the resistor.

bar wire wrapped round and soldered to pins

Transistors

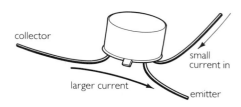

collector

small current in

larger current

emitter

A transistor is a special semi-conductor. It has three connections: a base, a collector and an emitter. When a small current is put on the base, it lets a much larger current flow between the collector and the emitter. So a tiny current can control a much larger one.

- Try this water-detector circuit.

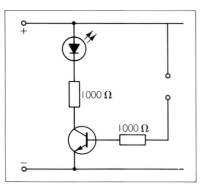

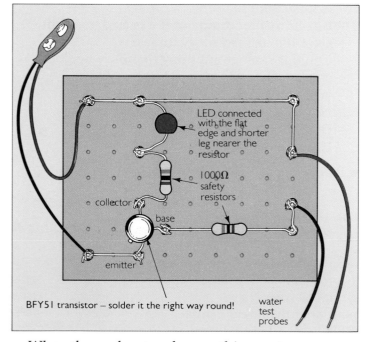

LED connected with the flat edge and shorter leg nearer the resistor

1000Ω safety resistors

collector

base

emitter

BFY51 transistor – solder it the right way round!

water test probes

When the probes touch something wet, a very small current goes from the battery through the water to the base of the transistor. This current is big enough to make the transistor work, so the LED lights up.

Printed circuits

Soldering makes better contacts than loose wires. The best connections of all are made with printed circuits. Printed circuits use very little wire. Instead, the circuit is printed in copper on a board.

● If you have etching equipment at school, you can try it, like this:

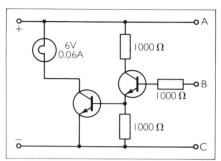

1. Look at the circuit diagram.

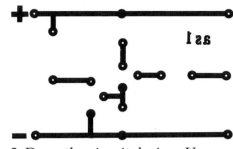

2. Draw the circuit design. Use transfer sheets or a black felt-tipped pen on an OHP transparency.

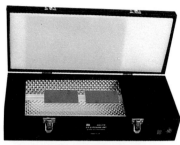

3. Put the transparency back to front on a piece of photo etch board. Expose it to ultra-violet light for 5 minutes. (**Care – eyes!**)

7. Wash the circuit in water. Wipe it with alcohol to clean off the remaining copper.

6. Etch it in acid iron (III) chloride to remove copper from the exposed areas (10–20 minutes). (**Care!**)

5. Wash the circuit in water.

4. Develop the exposed surface with 0.5 molar sodium hydroxide for 2 minutes. (**Care!**)

8. Drill the circuit.

9. Solder in the components (put the components on the fibreglass side and solder on the copper side). If you have no drill, you can mount the components straight on the copper side.

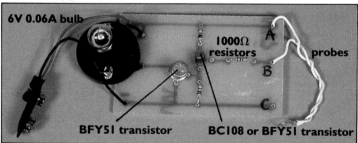

6V 0.06A bulb
1000Ω resistors
probes
A
B
C
BFY51 transistor
BC108 or BFY51 transistor

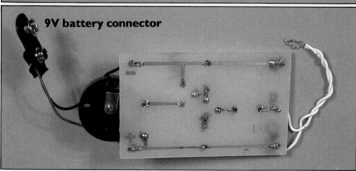

9V battery connector

The flowchart shows you how to make an etched circuit. The circuit in the example is called a Darlington pair. It is a very sensitive switch.

● Try it as a water detector by connecting probes to A and B.
● Try it as a light-detector by connecting a light-dependent resistor (LDR) between A and B, and a 1000 ohm resistor between B and C.
● Solder a second 1000 ohm resistor in parallel with (next to) the one between B and C. What difference does it make?
● Find out what happens if you put the LDR between B and C, and a 10 000 ohm resistor between A and B.

How it works

An LDR has a high resistance in the dark. When it is put in the light, its resistance drops. This makes the base of the first transistor positive, so it conducts. The first transistor then makes the second transistor conduct as well.

EXTRAS

1 Investigate your Darlington pair circuit with a voltmeter. Connect the minus terminal of the voltmeter to the minus line of the circuit. Connect the battery, but make sure the LED is off. Test and record the voltage at each point in the circuit using the voltmeter's + lead. Then turn the LED on and retest.

What differences did you find? Can you explain them?

2 (a) What equipment do you use that contains chips?
(b) How do you think your life would be different if microelectronics did not exist?

Try to imagine a world without paper. No books, no newspapers, no toilet paper . . .

Paper is vital to us because it is cheap and can be used in many different ways.

Paper is made from trees, mainly from spruce trees because they grow fast. One tree makes about 60kg of paper or 10 000 sheets of A4 paper. This is how paper is made.

In Britain we use about 8 million tonnes of paper each year. Half of this is made by recycling waste paper.

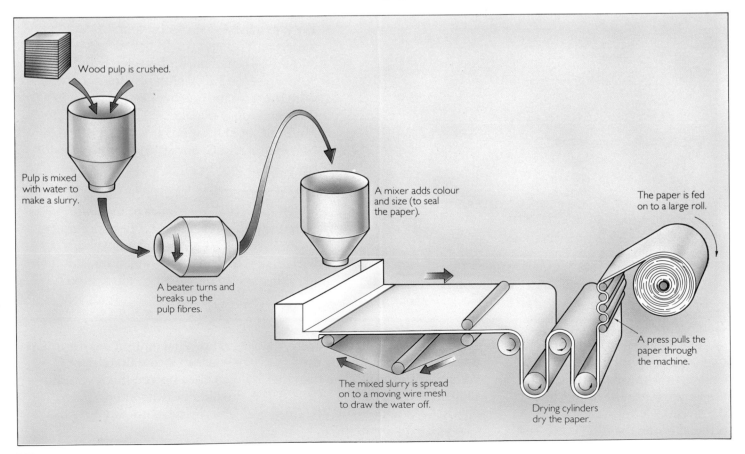

Wood pulp is crushed.

Pulp is mixed with water to make a slurry.

A beater turns and breaks up the pulp fibres.

A mixer adds colour and size (to seal the paper).

The mixed slurry is spread on to a moving wire mesh to draw the water off.

Drying cylinders dry the paper.

A press pulls the paper through the machine.

The paper is fed on to a large roll.

Testing paper

Wet strength

- Find out which type of tissue is strongest when wet.
- Write a report on your findings.
- Look at the best and worst tissues under a microscope.

1 What is it that makes a paper strong when it is wet?

Paper strength ⚠️

- Use one full-size newspaper and some string. You have to support a house-brick as high as possible off the ground.
- It is a good idea to plan the experiment and test the newspaper first. If you do not, you will waste a lot of time and paper. Take great care not to let the brick fall.

Card strength
Is corrugated card stronger than ordinary card?

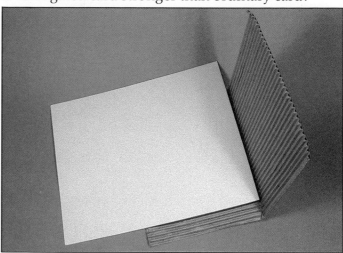

- Make a tube of the card you want to test. The tube should be about 5cm across and 15cm tall.
- Find out which type of card is stronger.

2 Does it matter if the corrugations go up the tube or round the tube?

Board strength

- Use scrap paper, scissors and flour or wallpaper paste (flour paste is made by mixing flour with water). You have to make a board of paper at least 20cm long and 20cm wide. It must not be more than 1cm thick.
- When your board is dry, find out what it will hold.

EXTRAS

1 The paper we use in Britain each year is made from 136 million trees.
(a) Where do all these trees come from?
(b) Spruce trees grow about 2 metres apart. What area would 136 million trees cover? (And remember that only 15 000 km² of Britain are heavily wooded.)

2 What is the tallest structure you can make from a single sheet of newspaper? It must stand up on its own without any support. You can use a little Sellotape to hold it together, but not to stick it to the ground.

3 Are we likely to need more or less paper in the future? Explain your answer.

Index